FRINGE, FRONT AND CENTER

Sermons For Sundays After
Pentecost (Middle Third)
Cycle B, Gospel Texts

George W. Hoyer

CSS Publishing Company, Inc., Lima, Ohio

FRINGE, FRONT AND CENTER

Copyright © 1996
CSS Publishing Company, Inc.
Lima, Ohio

All rights reserved. No part of this publication may be reproduced in any manner whatsoever without the prior permission of the publisher, except in the case of brief quotations embodied in critical articles and reviews. Inquiries should be addressed to: Permissions, CSS Publishing Company, Inc. P.O. Box 4503, Lima, Ohio 45802-4503

Scripture quotations are from the New Revised Standard Version of the Bible, copyright 1989 by the Division of Christian Education of the National Council of the Churches of Christ in the USA. Used by permission.

Library of Congress Cataloging-in-Publication Data

Hoyer, George W.
    Fringe, front and center : sermons for Sundays after Pentecost (middle third) : cycle B, Gospel texts / George W. Hoyer.
      p. cm.
    ISBN 0-7880-0801-3 (pbk.)
    1. Pentecost season — Sermons. 2. Sermons, American. 3. Bible. N.T. Gospels — Sermons. I. Title
BV4300.5.H68   1996
252'.6—dc20   96-4987
                                                                         CIP

This book is available in the following formats, listed by ISBN:
0-7880-0801-3   Book

PRINTED IN U.S.A.

To Dorothy
Gift of God

Table Of Contents

Preface — 7

Proper 10 — 9
    Look How You Listen
    Proper 10
    Mark 6:14-29 (C)

Pentecost 8 — 15
Ordinary Time 15
    Choose To Be Chosen
    Mark 6:7-13 (RC)

Proper 11 — 21
Pentecost 9
Ordinary Time 16
    What He Said!
    Mark 6:30-34, 53-56 (C)
    Mark 6:30-34 (RC)

Proper 12 — 27
Pentecost 10
Ordinary Time 17
    The Sign For Home
    John 6:1-21 (C)
    John 6:1-15 (RC)

Proper 13 — 33
Pentecost 11
Ordinary Time 18
    Bread In Our Baskets
    John 6:24-35

Proper 14 — 39
Pentecost 12
Ordinary Time 19
    Flesh For Our Life
    John 6:35, 41-51 (C)
    John 6:41-51 (RC)

Proper 15   43
Pentecost 13
Ordinary Time 20
   Himself The Real Presence
   John 6:51-58

Proper 16   49
Pentecost 14
Ordinary Time 21
   The Final Questions
   John 6:56-69 (C)
   John 6:60-69 (RC)

Proper 17   55
Pentecost 15
Ordinary Time 22
   Our Dilemma And Delight
   Mark 7:1-8, 14-15, 21-23

Proper 18   61
Pentecost 16
Ordinary Time 23
   Cheers For The Healed
   Mark 7:24-37 (C)
   Mark 7:31-37 (RC)

Proper 19   67
Pentecost 17
Ordinary Time 24
   The Taught Can
   Mark 8:27-38 (C)
   Mark 8:27-35 (RC)

Proper 20   73
Pentecost 18
Ordinary Time 25
   Last But Yet First
   Mark 9:30-37

Proper 21   79
Pentecost 19
Ordinary Time 26
   Children, Just Forever
   Mark 9:38-50 (C)
   Mark 9:38-43, 45, 47-48 (RC)

Lectionary Preaching After Pentecost   85

C — Revised Common Lectionary; RC — Roman Catholic Lectionary

Preface

All congregations, like all Gaul, are divided. Three parts that might be noted are the fringe, the front, and the center. Hearers sometimes space themselves — they sit in pews around the edges, in pews up front where the seeing and the hearing are better, or in the safely anonymous center.

Each person who hears a sermon is also divided. A part of each hearer is quite content to be there but to remain uncommitted. A part wishes to be somewhere else or for something other than a sermon offers. A blessed part is eager to hear, longing for fellowship with the Head and with members of the Body.

A sermon seeks to address all Gaul. The first goal is to be heard. How shall one preach without a hearer? A second part of the purpose of the sermon is to call a fringe a fringe, to unmask the center's complacency, and to help the front examine themselves. Where there is no known need there is no necessary solution. For all three the sermon is to be gospel. The good news is the power of God to attach the fringe, to move the center forward, to make the front pews the best seats in God's house.

Mark 6:14-29 (C)   Proper 10

Look How You Listen

The whole of today's gospel seems to be about John the Baptist. His death sentence was issued by Herod. His head was taken by a soldier of the guard. It was presented to Herodias on a platter and finally reached her mother who gloated over her revenge on the Baptizer.

Not to take anything else from John, still, the lesson today might be said to be not so much about John as it is about us. It is about us and how we hear. The dramatic and tragic details are all about the beheading of John the Baptist, but, it seems, Mark supplies that account only to explain Herod's reaction to what he was hearing about Jesus. That is the clue that today's message for us might well be what our Lord himself once said: "Take heed how ye hear." Look how you listen. Use your head to listen or you may lose more than your life.

Consider all this once again from that perspective. And before we begin, let me alert you to the conclusion I would suggest that we should reach. John lost his head but gained the kingdom. Unless we use our heads, we may lose the kingdom. Unless we put our minds to our hearing, we may lose the kingdom. But if we "when we hear the words of truth, the gospel of our salvation, believe on this Christ Jesus, we will be marked with the seal of the promised Holy Spirit, the pledge of our inheritance toward redemption as God's own people, to the praise of his glory" (Ephesians 1:13-14).

Now to the details. Notice how focused the text is on hearing. The first verse alerts us. "King Herod heard of it...." He heard how the twelve disciples were going about declaring that all should repent and casting out demons and anointing with oil and curing many who were sick.

Others were hearing the reports as well, "for Jesus' name had become known," this passage reports. And what is terribly serious and pertinent here for all of us is how these who *heard* reacted.

Some discounted the power of Jesus. They said, " 'John the Baptizer has been raised from the dead; and for this reason these powers are at work in him.' But others said, 'It is Elijah.' And others said, 'It is a prophet, like one of the prophets of old.' "

None of them really perceived God-in-Christ. None of them heard correctly. Jesus had not really become known to them. Matthew reports Jesus once said, "The reason I speak to them in parables is that seeing they do not perceive, and hearing they do not listen, nor do they understand" (Matthew 13:13).

There's the rub. There's the nub of the problem even today. See it in Herod in the way he listened to John. Herodias, the wife of Philip, his brother, whom he had married, had a grudge against John and wanted to kill him. But Herod "knowing that John was a righteous and holy man, protected him." Nevertheless, even though he perceived what kind of man John was, even though he listened to John, he didn't really hear and he certainly never understood. "When he heard him, he was greatly perplexed; and yet he liked to listen to him." What he had been hearing from John was certainly more than John's rebuking him because he had unlawfully married his brother's wife. This is what John was proclaiming — what his message is for us today. From his first appearance in the wilderness he proclaimed a baptism of repentance for the forgiveness of sins (Mark 1:4). And he announced the coming of Jesus who would "baptize with the Holy Spirit" (Mark 1:8). John baptized Jesus and testified, "I saw the Spirit descending like a dove, and it remained on him." The evangelist John reports his testimony. "I myself did not know him, but the one who sent me to baptize with water said to me, 'He on whom you see the Spirit descend and remain is the one who baptizes with the Holy Spirit.' And I myself have seen and have testified that this is the Son of God' " (John 1:32-34). Later, when John saw Jesus walking by, he said to his disciples, "Look, here is the Lamb of God!" (John 1:35).

Can we not conclude that John had said all these things to Herod as well? And Herod? Well, "he liked to listen to him." But he cut him short. Before he understood, he cut him short. The soldier of the guard beheaded him. But it was Herod who cut him short. John, who believed and confessed his faith in the Son of God, and who understood his words, "Do not fear those who kill the body but cannot kill the soul; rather fear him who can destroy both soul and body in hell" (Matthew 10:28), this John went headless to heaven. Herod, who liked to listen but was satisfied with being perplexed, went head-long to hell.

But keep remembering, this is about our hearing, *our* listening, *our* understanding. May I say *your* hearing, *your* listening, your understanding? May I say to you, all you who consider yourselves to be average Christians, who fill these pews Sunday after Sunday: Remember how easy it is to become accustomed to Christianity, no longer to be greatly moved by John's warning to flee from the wrath to come. Understand that we all are surrounded by evil and our wills remain weak because of sin. Are you actually regarding this Jesus as little more than "one of the prophets"? Are some even today not doing any better than Herod at really understanding?

This is about *your* hearing. As earnestly as I am able I say to any of you on the fringes of this congregation, who like to listen on occasional Sundays but are content to remain perplexed: Do not let John's message today fall short of your understanding. Let Herod be a warning. Perplexed, not persuaded, he let a foolish oath and a silly dancing girl destroy him. One cannot be saved even by much listening. He cut John off short and died short of believing.

The apostle Paul was treated in the same way as John. And finally his testimony was cut short just as was John's. When Paul was arrested and testified before the Roman governor, Felix, "concerning faith in Christ Jesus," and about "justice, self-control, and the coming judgment," Felix cut him short with the words, "Go away for the present, when I have an opportunity, I will send for you." To you who have been delaying your decision about Jesus Christ, as earnestly as I can I say, "Do not sell this Lord and Savior short." Felix "used to send for Paul very often and converse with him." But he left him in prison. One cannot be saved even by much listening (Acts 24:24-27).

Festus was the next governor, and he ordered Paul brought before his tribunal and invited King Agrippa and Bernice to sit in. When Paul defended himself and testified "that the Messiah must suffer and that, by being the first to rise from the dead, he would proclaim light both to our people and to the Gentiles" (Acts 26:23), Festus cut him short: "You are out of your mind, Paul!" And Paul turned to Agrippa: "King Agrippa, do you believe the prophets? I know you believe." But Agrippa cut him short: "Are you so quickly persuading me to become a Christian?" (Acts 26:27-28).

You who have only been listening and are perplexed, are you quickly becoming persuaded, or are you sitting fast? You who are temporizing and delaying your believing, hear, listen, and understand what Paul said to Agrippa. It is what the Spirit of God and I are saying to you now, "Whether quickly or not, I pray to God that not only you but also all who are listening to me today might become such as I am." This is what Paul *was*. He confessed, "Christ Jesus came into the world to save sinners, of whom I am the foremost." This is what Paul became: "But for that very reason, I received mercy, so that in me, as the foremost, Jesus Christ might display the utmost patience, making me an example to those who would come to believe in him for eternal life" (1 Timothy 1:15-16). This is what those Ephesians became of whom the Second Lesson speaks, "When you heard the words of truth, the gospel of your salvation, and had believed in him, you were marked with the seal of the promised Holy Spirit — the pledge of our inheritance toward redemption as God's own people."

Is not this what all of us, in our best desiring, want to become? All of us who have perceived in Jesus Christ the power and love of the Son of God, do we not long to be, fully and completely, beloved children of God? You who, like the twelve, have been following faithfully, do you not with the Ephesians say, "Blessed be the God and Father of our Lord Jesus Christ, who has blessed us in

Christ with every spiritual blessing ... just as he chose us in Christ ... to be holy and blameless before him in love" (Ephesians 1:1-4)? All of you, to whom again today God "has made known the mystery of his will according to his good pleasure ... set forth in Christ" (Ephesians 1:9), do you not feel the Spirit's urging to perceive, to hear, to understand, to receive him as your Savior, not only in your head but in your heart?

When Paul lost his head for Jesus' gospel and testimony, the Christians in Rome buried his body. And they continued as faithful followers even though he did not rise from the dead. When John's disciples heard about their teacher's death, "they came and took his body, and laid it in a tomb." And they believed John and followed the Lamb of God even though John did not rise from the dead. When Jesus breathed his last on the cross, and after the centurion said, "Truly this man was God's Son!" (Mark 15:39), then Joseph of Arimathea and others of Jesus' friends took down his body, wrapped it in a linen cloth, and laid it in a tomb (Mark 15:46).

But this Jesus *did* rise from the dead! On the third day Joseph — and you and I — believed the message of the angels, "He has been raised!" On the third day they — and you and I — perceived him: "Behold! it is I myself!" They listened: "It was necessary that the Messiah should suffer and rise from the dead that repentance and forgiveness of sins be proclaimed to all!" They understood when they gathered around his table and heard him say, "Take eat, take drink — my body, my blood, given for you!" They — and you and I! If Herod, perplexed, feared because he thought John had been raised from the dead, how much more do we, we who are wise to salvation and know our Lord *is* risen from the dead and has gone before us to glory, how much more should each one of us say, each day, "Just as I am, Oh, Lamb of God, I come! I come!"

Mark 6:7-13 (RC)   Pentecost 8
Ordinary Time 15

Choose To Be Chosen

What a relief to be chosen! Remember? When the captains began to choose up sides for a softball game? That terrible feeling that you might be the last one chosen or not be chosen at all? "The rest of you can just go out in the outfield somewhere"...or "The rest of you can sit on the sidelines and we'll substitute you later on".... But when you *were* chosen, perhaps even sixth or seventh, then it was over. You were *in*! What a relief!

"God chose us in Christ before the foundation of the world." That's the good news in today's Second Lesson. What a relief to know that! The twelve chosen apostles help us comprehend the greatness of that blessing in today's gospel. You did not, you could not, do that choosing. That is God's doing. But now — once chosen — we can choose to be chosen. We can choose to live as the chosen. That is a way of saying we can exercise our election. We can get into the game. We can score. We can choose to be chosen.

But back to that feeling of "will I be chosen?" In honesty, many of us must admit that the reason we were so haunted by the fear we might not be chosen was that we really were not very good. Of course, that wasn't so for some of you. Some of you were always good at games, all the games. And so some of you might not be on this wave length at all about how good it is to be chosen, even if only for right field. Of course, what we're talking about here is more serious than softball. The subject is about players on God's field and the question is "Who can be on God's side?" May I risk again speaking directly to those of you who have been content to sit on the sidelines of the Church, who have not yet agreed to try for the team? It is not enough to think you are good enough to play if you simply decide to do so. For one thing, God does the choosing. For another God sets the criteria. Remember John the Baptist's words to his countrymen who thought they were the best? "You brood of vipers! Who warned you to flee from the wrath to come?" (Matthew 3:7). Let him who thinketh he can bat 300 take heed lest he striketh out. The rules are by God. And by God and only by God are we rated. So this matter of being chosen is of eternal concern to every man, woman, and child. Think seriously then about what a blessing it is to be chosen by this God with whom we have to do.

Consider the twelve, the chosen twelve, fisherfolk, a tax man, no one exceptional. What made them special was that they were chosen by the Son of God. Don't you suppose they had known discouragement before? And surely they must have felt discouraged afterwards. Here Jesus sent them out two by two into the villages to proclaim that all should repent. But our Lord allowed for discouragement — "If any will not welcome you and they refuse to hear you, as you leave, shake off the dust that is on your feet as a testimony against them." Certainly a help — permission to vent one's spleen. But what is back of that is the reminder, "You are chosen. I chose you. Who are these people who reject those whom I have chosen? Are you going to take their reaction to you above my choosing you?" Are you? You can now choose to be chosen because God has chosen you. If God be for us, what difference does it make who is against us? So what if you are but "a herdsman and a dresser of sycamore trees" as was Amos, the prophet in today's First Lesson? The Lord took you! The things that discourage us are not worthy to be compared to the wonder of our being chosen. Choose to live as the chosen!

Or think about those times when you think you are not good enough for God to keep on liking you. Perhaps you have even allowed yourself to be persuaded that all the trouble you've been seeing is evidence that God is punishing you. Probably you're not even a child of God, you may say to yourself. Don't doubt. It's official! "He destined us for adoption as his children through Jesus Christ!" our lesson assures us. Adopted children can find a place among siblings with the confidence that they were *chosen*. They were not merely born "of blood or of the will of the flesh or of the will of man," as scripture says of us (John 1:13). They — we — were chosen, born of God. How ridiculous for any of us then to strive for a kind of parthenogenesis, for an "I did it my way" status, as if we had given birth to ourselves. "You did not choose me," says our God. "You couldn't. But I have chosen you!" Relax and rejoice that we are among the chosen. Choose to be chosen!

That was at the heart of the message which the twelve were sent to proclaim to "the chosen people." They were confused in different ways about their chosen-ness. These were Old Testament believers in Jahweh. What good news for Jews could those apostles relate? "Repent," said the duo of apostles. "At whose supreme command?" asked the villagers. "Jesus of Nazareth" would have been the answer. And thus the message of the apostles became the same as that which the Lord himself had been proclaiming in Galilee. "Repent and believe in the good news" (Mark 1:15). The best of the good news is Jesus. Jesus is the proof of our chosen-ness.

Jesus was not yet telling his disciples everything. This was still early on in their training. And early on in our Lord's redeeming work. He had scarce begun to do the proclaiming that he had come from the Father as the promised Messiah, had scarce begun his dying role, had the tomb and three days in death before his resurrection to life again. These disciples could not relate all that we know about God's plan for salvation. Now everything has been revealed to us. Think of what any one of us could have added to what these disciples said had we been one of a pair who entered a villager's house. To whatever the apostle said we would be able to say, "And what's more..." and we could use all that today's Second Lesson has spelled out as our text.

Here are some of those lines anew. "The God of our fathers" they knew. Now *we* bless the God and Father of our Lord Jesus — the only Son of the Father, sent by him to accomplish our choosing and our adoption. They depended on the promised blessing to Abraham, Isaac, and Jacob. We know the seed promised as the one by whom all nations blessed themselves to be Jesus. God has blessed us in Christ. God chose us in Christ before the foundation of the world. They boasted Abraham as their father — they were the children of Abraham. We are God's children through Jesus Christ. They knew themselves as the people of the law. We give all power to God's grace for our choosing, our predestining according to the good pleasure of his will. God's glorious grace has been bestowed on us through the Beloved Son. They looked back to the exodus, the wanderings, and the conquest of Canaan as evidence of their chosen-ness. We know of the redemption of the world, planned before time began, accomplished in the fullness of time — when Jesus Christ shed his blood for our salvation, the forgiveness of our trespasses, lavished on us by divine grace. All of this, once a mystery, God has revealed to us by his good pleasure. He has given us all wisdom and insight into how through Christ we obtain an eternal inheritance. And for right now, when we hear this word of truth, the gospel of our salvation, we who set our hope on Christ are enabled to live for the praise of his glory. We can choose to be chosen. As a guarantee of all this, we have been marked with the seal of the Holy Spirit, a pledge of our inheritance as God's own people. We have been baptized and marked with the sign of his cross forever. We are chosen. We can now choose to be chosen.

What now are we to do? Of course, we, too, have been chosen by God to be witnesses to all these things. But what we are to do above all and first of all is exactly what the twelve told the people in the villages to do: "Repent and believe!" Believe that God has indeed chosen you in Christ Jesus to be his child and heir. Accept your being chosen. And repent — that is far more than saying, "Sorry," far more than "promising to do better." Repenting implies acknowledging that we cannot choose ourselves, accepting the good news that we have been chosen and accepted by God. Humankind's most grievous fault is the arrogance which claims it can play life's game on its own. The hundred percent turnaround which is repentance is confessing that it is only by grace, by God's choosing and enabling, that we can participate in life as God wills it to be lived. Repentance means accepting the good news that we have been chosen and accepted by God, and seeking God's coaching to play life's game as God wants it played.

Believe it! You're on the team. Choose now to be a chosen one. Wear your uniform, the righteousness God gives you through Christ Jesus, gratefully. Get out early for extra practice on the field — a workout with Word and prayer. Realize the blessing of God's food at the training table. You need never be discouraged, never need to feel you'll be traded if you make errors. Yours is an eternal contract. Choose to live as the chosen one you are!

Anyone who supplied free room and board for messengers who brought this good news surely got a bargain.

Now it is ours, this certainty of being chosen, without money and without price. What a bargain! For us to live in Christ and even to die is a bargain. What a blessed choice, to choose to be chosen!

Mark 6:30-34, 53-56 (C) Proper 11
Mark 6:30-34 (RC) Pentecost 9
Ordinary Time 16

What He Said!

People left his presence marvelling — this Jesus — they left his great gatherings amazed. "What he said!" *they* said.

In today's gospel we are not told if our Lord actually said it, or whether he simply thought it: "They are like sheep without a shepherd." Modern medicine has an amazing diagnostic tool called Magnetic Resonance Imagining — MRI. The machine provides the magnetic magic and computers translate it all into pictures sharper than X-ray. Whether Jesus thought it or said it, what we have here is the Messiah's Reaction Imagery: "They are like sheep without a shepherd."

The disciples had returned from their teaching trips through the villages. They reported to *their* Teacher. Their experiences must have ranged from tearful acceptances of the good news and of Jesus as the promised Messiah to outright rejection of their message and even ridicule of their persons. Now, here in this once deserted spot, they found themselves surrounded by a mixed mob of people, some hoping to see miracles, some suffering and sick, all hoping for healing, all pressing to see Jesus. And his MRI — his Messianic Imaging? "They are like sheep without a shepherd."

For good or for ill, the shepherd-sheep analogy is a much-used biblical image. In the First Lesson (Jeremiah 23:1-6) today the prophet Jeremiah places that comparison in the mouth of "the Lord, the God of Israel." Saint Mark in today's gospel places the same figure of speech in the mouth of the Son of this Lord, the God of Israel. In Jeremiah God condemns those "shepherds who destroy and scatter" the people of God. God promises to gather the scattered sheep and to raise up shepherds who will do a good job of shepherding. In Mark Jesus sees God's task is not yet finished because the people of God were still "like sheep without a shepherd." Clearly, it is hard to get good shepherds and harder to keep them on the job.

But Psalm 23 makes the Lord himself the shepherd. And, of course, Jesus names himself the "Good Shepherd." Saint John writes that Jesus came to his own people and his own did not receive him. This is the greatest evidence that the mission of Jesus was vital; namely, to gather the lost sheep of the house of Israel (Matthew 15:25). In the Psalm the sheep knew their shepherd and realized that only with the shepherd's care could they want nothing. But what of those of us who know no shepherd?

May I say a word once more directly to those among us today who linger on the fringe of the flock, who are not ready to confess that this Lord, this Jesus Christ, "is *my* shepherd"? In all probability you, and most all of us, will acknowledge that we do not feel "sheepish" about our relationship with God. The imagery is not the most helpful for our age. But the vital situation God is making clear to us remains terribly important. "Sheep without a shepherd" describes all whose relationship with God has broken down or is non-existent. That is today's issue. Whether shepherds all did a poor job of shepherding in your case, or as sheep you deliberately scattered, or, poor lambs, you never seem to have had a shepherd or been introduced to God the good shepherd, all that is beside the point at this stage. But alienation from God is a terrible, tragic problem.

For us to realize what scatteredness, what shepherdlessness, what alienation from God means, we might do well to translate all this sheep-shepherd imagery into current terms. From God's point of view every created thing ought to realize that only in God do we live, move, and have being. Of course, there may be some here who do not admit the existence of God. Some of you may not concede that the concept "God" by definition makes that Being the source and the strength and the ultimate satisfaction of life. But the fact that you are here, even if only on the fringe of Church life, suggests that you do operate at least somewhat on the premise that God exists and that this God has definite relationships with all of us human beings. Come, then, let us reason together in contemporary terms.

Imagine one of those huge trailer trucks which carry six or seven new cars from the factory to your auto dealer's showroom. Those cars were made to be your helper, your servant. You arrive to make one your own, say the red convertible. You are ready to love, honor, and polish it, only to discover that it has this prejudice against gasoline. "I think it stinks. It may cause cancer. One spark and it might explode all over me." What to do? You could abandon it. You could try to reason with it. Beat on it, perhaps.

Now see this Jesus crossing the lake in a boat and coming to a deserted place with his disciples. And whom does he meet? Us. Us without a clue about what turns us over. Us with an aversion to the one thing which gives us life, liberty, and happiness. What is Jesus to do? In him dwells all wisdom and knowledge. By him all things were made. He himself, made as a man, as human as you and I, with arms, legs, organs, brains. The only thing we have he doesn't have is sin. Here he arrives, right off the boat, and discovers us. Some of us have the sheep's biggest problem — not recognizing the shepherd. Some of us refuse to acknowledge our servanthood. Some scorn or ridicule the theory that gasoline makes the car go round. What did he do then? And now? "He began to teach them many things." What can we learn?

Today's Second Lesson (Ephesians 2:13-22) spells out a great deal of the "many things" Jesus revealed. He surely did not try to teach all of this, then, to those people. God has taught much of this to many of you — and you will rejoice to hear it all anew. But even if some of you are not all that ready to hear all the details or the mechanics of what Jesus Christ has accomplished for this world, at least focus on what a great guy Jesus is. That was the most astounding of the many things he must have taught them — that God, almighty, omnipotent God, *cares,* and not only deeply cares, but, truly, God is present, God is *here.* His very *being there* said, "You don't want to miss out on this. You can know God and you can have God's love and care and you can find meaning and purpose in life. Restless? Of course you are — until you who were made by God, for God, find rest in God." "Come unto me," Jesus said, "and you will find rest!"

He taught them many things. Without God in the world you are without hope. But now God, coming to us in the flesh-and-blood Jesus Christ, has brought us near. God created this "nearness" by *being* near. "He is our peace!"

Much of Ephesians 2:13-22 describes how God-in-Christ has broken down the wall which divided Gentiles and Jews. But it also describes how the wall separating us from God has been broken down, and how God deeply desires to destroy the wall which still divides your heart from God's heart. Hear it that way. Hear more of the many things our Lord taught.

In his flesh-and-blood presence God has broken down the dividing wall of hostility between us and God. To know God-in-Christ is to love God. He has abolished the law which said that if you sin you die. Instead *he* died. God-in-Christ died and now, by his grace, even though you sin, you are forgiven. God has reconciled all of us to God through the cross, "putting to death that hostility through it." So he came and proclaimed peace — proclaims now — peace to you who were far off and to you who are near. Through him all of us have access in one Spirit to the Father. "So then you are no longer strangers and aliens, but you are citizens with the saints and also members of the household of God."

It's accomplished. It's done. You are *in*. Accept it! Believe it! Be glad about it!

There were many things Jesus did not teach that crowd then. He hadn't yet done many of the things he had come to do. Much of his teaching, all of his dying, his triumphant resurrection, are still in the future. But the essence of it all was there — for *he* was there. God was in Christ loving; God was in Christ reconciling the world. And by Messianic Imagery Jesus made that clear. You bring your sick loved one on a mat to him in some marketplace and he touches the one you love and he heals your child, your wife, your husband. Do you doubt that God has come near, that God loves? Of course,

God has not done anything like that for many of you, and many of you have asked time and time again. But Jesus did not heal everyone then, and he didn't even touch China or England, not to mention North America. God didn't even spare the Beloved Son the evil which sin has brought down upon us all. But when God delivered up that Son of God for us it has become certain that nothing like death nor illness nor things present nor things to come can separate us from the love of God in Christ Jesus our Lord!

Well. Start your motors. Obviously Jesus would not have tried the automobile-gasoline analogy for that crowd. But he did work with the food analogy. He taught that we could not live on bread alone, but he fed that whole bunch after his sermon. And our Lord is prepared to do the food bit anew for us here. He takes this bread and promises, "My body." He takes this wine and promises, "My blood." And always repeats his promise, "Given and shed for you for the forgiveness of sins." Do this in remembrance, for the remembrance, of him. And run with it!

John 6:1-21 (C)   Proper 12
John 6:1-15 (RC)   Pentecost 10
                                                       Ordinary Time 17

The Sign For Home

The crowd gathered because they saw the signs Jesus was doing for the sick. Another sign was the meal for the thousands. But among the thousands there were different interpretations of that sign. Some said it showed that Jesus was the long-awaited prophet God had promised Israel. Others said it showed that in any election Jesus would be a shoe-in for king.

Outdated political bumper stickers are, of all signs, surely the most irrelevant. "Thomas E. Dewey for President" is as meaningful as "Tippecanoe and Tyler Too." But up-to-date significant signs go unheeded at great cost: "Bridge out" or "Detour." They are vital signs. They are signs that affect life or death. Signs determine whether you make it home or get where you're going. The sign in today's gospel is significant, vital for today.

Jesus was the sign maker. He was creating these signs on purpose. Jesus knew what he was doing. Hear verse six again: "He himself knew what he was going to do." The verse seems to call for parentheses. Jesus had seen the large crowd and said to Philip, "Where are we to buy bread for these people to eat?" Then — think parentheses — verse six: "This he said to test him, for he himself knew what he was going to do." Close parentheses. Some interpreters call this verse a scribal addition, added to make sure readers would not get the impression that his question indicated that Jesus did *not* know what he was doing.

From where we believers sit, here, after all the facts of salvation history are in, we can say Jesus was doing everything here *on purpose*. He knew that his signs, that is, his healing of the sick, were attracting crowds. On purpose, then, he took up his position with disciples on this little mountain by the sea. "When he looked up" — those words, as we read them, almost suggest that he did that on purpose, too, that he made a contrived move of surprise that conveyed a meaning like, "Why, look at that! A great crowd is coming." Then he asked the question, "Where are we to buy bread for these people to eat?" He did not ordinarily take the responsibility for providing a free lunch for the crowds that came out to see him. Here was another mixed crowd of onlookers, gawkers, and the curious, of honest seekers, unbelievers, and many who were sick. All of them were needy, Jesus knew, but many did not know how needy they really were. What sort of sign would help them realize what was really going on here in Palestine at Passover time to meet their need? Why would Jesus even suggest the possibility of feeding them all? He did it on purpose, don't you think?

Jesus knew what he was doing. He was speaking to Israel — and to us — in sign language. John underlines *signs* when he describes the miraculous acts Jesus performed, from the changing of water into wine on through the healing of the nobleman's son and the healing on the sabbath of the man hoping for health at the pool of Bethesda. In this section we have heard John call what Jesus was doing for the sick *signs*. At the close of today's gospel account the feeding of the 5,000 is called a sign: "When the people saw the *sign* that he had done...." Sign language.

Jesus knew what he was doing. He was himself a sign. Here he appears to be deliberately setting up a sign that would publicize the fact that God was behind all that he did. God was being revealed in the person and the performances of Jesus. He — Jesus — was an in-the-flesh revelation of God, his divine Father. And this feeding of the multitude was designed as a sign to show the people of Israel that if they liked Moses, they really ought to *love* Jesus, the Messiah. This sign was a proclamation that one greater than Moses had appeared.

Our greatest danger would be to glance at this sign as if it were an outdated sort of bumper sticker. It is a vital sign for us today, even as it was back then. Focus on the meaning of that sign and take it to heart. All the rest is detail, the 5,000 head count, the two dried fish. Of course, there was more to the significance of the loaves over which Jesus gave thanks and which he distributed. John is not only recording the fact that Jesus said "grace" before lunch. We will hear the echo of that blessing later when we prepare our table for another of our Lord's bread blessings. In fact, we will think more about that in the next four Sundays as the gospels record Jesus' claim to be the bread from heaven. But for now, focus on the meaning of this sign. It shows us the way home.

Try to see this as God sees it. God had been setting up signs for home ever since the first couple had been put out of their home in Eden. Thorns and thistles were signs that going against God's directives could only mean disaster. The flood was a sign more obvious than "Bridge Out." Abraham and Sarah had Isaac for a sign and all that happened to Jacob and his "children of Israel" was God's sign of a new homeward way which was to come. The standout sign language came in the life and deeds of Moses. The exodus from Egypt was so clearly a sign of God's favor that Moses and Elijah at the Lord's transfiguration discussed Jesus's saving passion as his exodus which he would accomplish in Jerusalem. But it was Moses himself who clued Israel in on the sign developed in today's gospel. Before his death Moses reminded Israel that God had told him, "I will raise up for them a prophet like you" (like Moses, that is) "from among their own people; I will put my words into the mouth of the prophet, who shall speak to them everything that I command (Deuteronomy 18:17-18)." After our Lord's resurrection, Peter made the sign connection of "that prophet" and Jesus clear to the Israelites of his day and also to us. In Solomon's portico he and John had healed a man lame from birth. They told the crowd that it was the name of Jesus which empowered the miracle. And then Peter identified Jesus with the prophet whom God would raise up, even as Moses had said (Acts 3:22f).

What Jesus was doing here for these thousands was being done on purpose, for this purpose: to alert them to what God was doing to bring them to the eternal promised land. What would come to people's minds when a large crowd in a desert place was miraculously given all the food they could eat and then some? Moses, of course! Moses gave Israel God's gifts of manna and quail in the wilderness. In the strength of that miraculous food they followed Moses to the promised land. And who was doing it now? Jesus was. And what was the meaning of the sign? That one greater than Moses had appeared, the promised prophet, who was speaking for God, who would accomplish a greater exodus than Moses, who would bring them to a better home than Canaan.

Clearly the value of a sign depends upon the correct interpretation. People got the point of this one, all right. Those of the crowd who thought the Messiah's role was to free them from Roman rule wanted to take him by force and make him king. Jesus withdrew, practically fled, to disabuse them of that dream in a hurry. Those who correctly interpreted the sign said, "This is indeed the prophet who is to come into the world."

We, too, should be sure our understanding of this sign is correct. It is a vital sign. God chose Israel as his own people to make them a sign for all the world, a light to the Gentile nations, a sign that God was for real, that God was involved with human life, that God loved even an erring people. God rescued Israel from bondage as a sign that this "Greater than Moses" would rescue all people from the slavery of sin and evil. Jesus knew what he was doing when he performed this sign. At issue is whether *we* all realize what Jesus was doing. And at issue after that is whether we do something about what Jesus has done.

And this is what we should do. It's as simple as what the hungry thousands did when Jesus distributed the bread he had blessed: they took it and said, "Thank you, Jesus." What God-in-Christ is distributing today to all of us, to all the world, is the forgiveness of all our sins. We take it and say, "Thank you, O Savior." What he is offering to us today is life, true life, abundant life for each today, and salvation for the eternity of life which will follow our dying. What we do is receive it, live it, share it and say, "Thank you, our Lord and Friend!" Even a child knows what to do when offered bread: take, eat, be satisfied, grow by it. And when by a sign like this miracle God offers us forgiveness, life, and salvation, surely we "sign on"; we receive it; we give thanks.

Jesus, who knew then what he was doing, and knows now, tells us again, "Take and eat." That crowd received his gifts and was satisfied. We, too, who eat of this bread which he blesses and taste of this cup which he offers, know that the Lord is good!

Some bumpers carry a sign that says, "If you can read this, you're too close. Back off." This Sunday's sign says, "If you understand this, you're very near the Kingdom. Come closer." Come nearer. He is the sign. Read him: "I am the way. By me you come to the Father. Listen to me. Follow me. Follow me home!"

John 6:24-35   Proper 13
Pentecost 11
Ordinary Time 18

Bread In Our Baskets

After the Lord's miraculous multiplying of the two fish and the loaves of bread, the crowd had seen the disciples shove off for the farther shore. They knew there had been only one boat by the shore. They knew Jesus had not entered it with the disciples. Do you suppose some in the crowd said to one another, "Jesus missed the boat"? Those who wanted to make Jesus king might have said that and meant that he could have become a great deal more than he was. They didn't realize that no one ever was greater than he. Nor did they realize that without him they were the ones who were missing the boat.

John's account describes the disciples' crossing. They had rowed three or four miles across and found it rough going indeed, with the strong wind and high waves. Suddenly they saw Jesus walking on the sea, coming near them. They were terrified. "It is I," he said. "Do not be afraid." When Moses wanted to know God's name so that he could identify who was sending him to rescue the children of Israel in Egypt, God had told him, "I AM WHO I AM" (Exodus 3:14). He is who he is, the Son of God. "I am the one greater than Moses. *He* divided the sea for Israel's crossing. *I* rise above it. I make it my footstool. I walk on it." The disciples wanted him to get into the boat, but the text does not tell us that he did. Instead — "Immediately the boat reached the land toward which they were going." Jesus didn't miss the boat. He controlled it. And all who were in the boat he brought to shore. It's the boat none of us wants to miss.

The day after the miracle meal, some of the great crowd were evidently still at the mountain. They piled into some new boats which had come from Tiberias and crossed the sea to Capernaum where they found Jesus. The first question they put to him was, "Rabbi, when did you come here?" What they probably wondered about was "How did you get here?" What would have been their reaction if Jesus had replied to their curiosity, "I walked." What they really needed to learn was the answer to the question, "Who are you — really?" What is *our* reaction to the answer we have heard — "I AM"? What are we doing about his words, "I am the bread of life"?

Clearly the crowd didn't know what in the world Jesus was doing, what he was doing for the world. Jesus at once put it to them that they were missing the boat. He underlined his words with a "verily." "Very truly, I tell you, you are looking for me, not because you saw signs, but because you ate your fill of the loaves. Do not work for the food that perishes, but for the food that endures for eternal life." Our Lord's "very truly" makes this charge a very serious one, and one which we do well to heed today. Do we react truly to the sign of the loaves? Do we *verily* work for the food that endures for eternal life?

Think about some of them in *that* crowd who were missing the boat. That's easier than critically examining ourselves. With that huge more-than-five-thousand crowd, there were, no doubt, some stragglers at the fringes who arrived late and asked, "What's going on? Why the crowd?"

"Bread and fish!" was their answer. "Jesus and the disciples are passing out bread and fish. Sit down here on the grass."

"Don't mind if I do. Who said there's no such thing as a free lunch?"

"The word is that Jesus blessed the lunch a little boy brought along, and he's stretching it out for all these thousands. What a prophet! It's like manna."

"Tastes like fish to me."

It would have been people like that who clambered aboard the boats to follow the disciples to Capernaum. It would have been to people like that that Jesus had to say sadly, "Very truly, I tell you, you are looking for me because you ate your fill of the loaves." But, brothers and sisters, "I would not have you to be ignorant" that there are fringes to our congregational crowd as well, and there are very probably people here who have been wandering on the edges of the Church for months, for years. Many people find many reasons for joining the Church crowd, reasons which have little to do with the serious issues of death, of life after death, of sin which puts God off, or of how God can be expected to react toward those who ignore him. Some readily appropriate the side advantages of being churchly, things like respectability, standing for moral and ethical values, hearing good music, or experiencing the good feeling of doing what your mother told you to do. But to any like that, to any of you who are on the fringe like that, content with lunch, not interpreting the sign, not comprehending the gift or recognizing the Giver, Jesus is speaking today. "You are missing the boat," Jesus is saying.

Jesus hoped that people would see the sign and come looking for him for a rescue greater than Moses ever offered, for a prophet not only sent by God, but actually God! Jesus hoped that by giving them the bread that perished as they ate it, they would come looking for him to receive from him the bread of eternal life, to receive what no Moses could ever give — the eternal promised land, true life here, flowing with divine milk and honey. Giving out food for thousands was no big distribution problem for the Son of God, for God regularly satisfies the desires of every living thing. But, clearly, it was food that perishes. Even the twelve baskets that remained probably met the same fate the next day. What Jesus hoped for was that these people — what Jesus *hopes* for — is that all of us, in the front rows, in the safe center, on the fringes, would come to him for "the food that endures for eternal life, which the Son of Man gives. For it is on him that God the Father has set his seal."

The crowd by now had probably increased by hundreds from this new parish area around Capernaum. They had missed the miracle and so pressed him to give them a sign "so that we may see it and believe you." "How about showing *us* something," they were saying, "something equal to the manna Moses gave? 'Bread from heaven' the scriptures call it." Jesus replied, "It wasn't Moses who gave bread from heaven, but my Father who gives you the true bread from heaven. For the bread of God is that which comes down from heaven and gives life to the world."

Finally the people gave him the reaction he wanted. "They said to him, 'Sir, give us this bread always.' " Even though it was still not clear that they were understanding what he meant, Jesus made his point explicit: "I am the bread of life. Whoever comes to me will never be hungry, and whoever believes in me will never be thirsty." "Come to me; believe in me." That sums up his answer to the question, "What must we do to perform the works of God?" Here he tells us, too, what we are to do: "This is the work of God, that you believe in him whom he has sent."

There it is, clearly said, to all of us in front and center and fringe. He was not yet putting it all in words, all that he had agreed with his Father to do. He came to give life to the world. "Bread of life" was his illustration of all that he was offering to all of us. Bread must be consumed in order to give life. We must consume, we must believe, we must swallow, all that Jesus has told us, all that Jesus has done for us if we would have true life. This is the work God wants us to do.

The work of God which the Father wanted Jesus to do was to be consumed in death. The sin which kills could itself be killed only by God's taking its death into the divine being. And the divine being could only partake of death by taking on our humanity. God raised up Jesus, a prophet like Moses also in this, as a child of Israel, a child of Mary, a child like us. In the mind of Jesus there could have been a connection other than bread to the work of Moses. Moses died before Israel made it to the promised land. Death was to be a part of our Lord's work as well. Jesus died to enable us to make it to the promised land. Moses died for his own sin. Jesus died for ours. No one knows where Moses' grave is. There is no point in looking for Jesus' grave. He is not in it. He is risen indeed.

All of that, his obedience to the Father, his death for us for our failures, his new life for his friends, make up the ingredients of the bread of life. All that God's recipe called for, the whole mix of the works and the word of Jesus, make up the bread of life. And Jesus slices it simply for us, gives us the whole loaf in one piece: "I am the bread of life. Believe in me whom God has sent." Oh, that each one of us would realize how wonderful a gift Jesus gives to us! We have tasted the miracle of the Bread of Life. For years we have feasted out of the leftovers gathered in the twelve baskets. And look in your basket right now. There is more than a bit of fish and a bit of bread there!

Think of it through the little boy's eyes. It would be pleasing to us all, I think, if we could know that the little boy managed to get a seat on one of the boats which followed Jesus. Say his name was Thaddaeus...call him Tad. It would be pleasing to think of him as he worked his way to the front of the crowd to a place where he could see Jesus plainly. Pleasing to think that Jesus recognized him, called him by name, said, "Tad! Glad you could come. Won't need your lunch today." And then Jesus notices that Tad's basket is empty today — no fish, no bread; just his faith, his work of God, his belief in him whom God has sent.

Then Jesus, aware now of the empty basket, quietly says, "Nothing in your lunch basket today, Tad? Well, then. A special blessing, just for you." And now, in the basket, a small dried fish, two little barley loaves, and ... a little frosted cupcake.

"More than we can ask or think!" That is what our Lord is giving to us who believe. Pleasing it was to God to give us the savior Son. Pleasing it is to our God, now, that we bring to him our offertory basket of bread and wine. Pleasing it is to our God to bless us and these gifts, and place anew into our hands and lives, the **Bread of Life!**

John 6:35, 41-51 (C)
John 6:41-51 (RC)

Proper 14
Pentecost 12
Ordinary Time 19

Flesh For Our Life

Once again our Lord tells us, "I am the living bread that came down from heaven." "Bread of life" — that metaphor sums up all that Jesus said and did. "Whoever eats of this bread will live forever," Jesus says. That "eating" metaphor about the "bread" metaphor describes our grasp of faith by which we appropriate for ourselves all that God-in-Christ has said and done for us. Now Jesus tells us more: "The bread that I will give for the life of the world is my flesh." That is what he said. And all that he has done for us began when "the Word became flesh and lived among us" (John 1:14). That flesh was real. Ask Mary who first checked the toes on the little feet of the Holy Child and felt the tight grasp of his hand. Our Lord Jesus, the Son of God in our flesh, revealed God's glorious love in what he said and in what he did. What he said he was able to say only because he was made flesh. What he did he was able to do only because he was made flesh. Jesus is our Savior in the flesh. He gave that flesh, he gave himself for the life of the world.

People were put off by what he said — words about being "the bread of life" and "coming down from heaven." But they were drawn to him by what he did. Remember: "I, when I am lifted up from the earth, will draw all people to myself" (John 12:32).

First, think about what he said. This was flesh talking. This was a human tongue in a human body proclaiming. As we listen anew to some things he said, we can feel for these Jews who murmured, "Is not this Jesus, the son of Joseph, whose father and mother we know? How can he now say, 'I have come down from heaven'?" And, of course, that was not all that gave, that gives, hearers difficulty. He said, "My Father, God, is back of all this. My Father sent me. Only if my Father draws you, can you manage to be on my side. Even the scriptures tell you that when they say you have to be 'taught by God.' You have to hear and learn from the Father, then you can come to me. Not that you can expect to see the Father. Only I can, only I have, I who came from the Father. But, believe me, whoever believes has eternal life. Manna didn't keep your ancestors alive. But I am the bread that comes down from heaven so that one may eat of it and not die."

People were put off by his words. And not only those people. People on the fringes of our crowd here, even people in the front rows, some of the time even people in the center pews murmur, "Can this all really be true?" Popular wisdom has it that "some things just can't be put into words." God doesn't agree, of course. As his Son said, "Everyone who has heard and learned from the Father comes to me." God took to himself in his Son human flesh, human nature, the better to put into words his love for his creatures, his plan to reconcile them to himself. Speech is a distinguishing mark of all of us who are of human flesh. The Word was made flesh to give us words of life. We ought to rejoice that God gave us the Word made flesh, that Jesus used his flesh to give us words of life. He said, "I am the bread of life." He gave us himself, in what he said. He gave "his flesh for the life of the world."

Now think about what he did, how God in flesh made God's love real to us by what he did. "No one can come to me unless drawn by the Father," Jesus said. And how did the Father propose to do that drawing? Yes, by a drawing, by a picture worth the Word, by making himself accessible to our sight, to our touch, as well as to our hearing, by living among us in flesh.

Think about that flesh, his flesh, our Lord's flesh. Do you suppose Jesus ever marvelled at his own flesh? He who was both God and man, and knew it. Well, of course we cannot possibly know how he thought about being incarnate as one born in flesh. He who had seen God, had thought it no arrogance to claim equality with God, who had come from God, who was God — did he ever consider how far beyond all possible human expectation it was for people to experience God walking around on two feet, eating bread, drinking wine, touching a little girl's hand to lift her up alive on her death bed, reaching for the little boy's basket, distributing the bread and fish? What a marvelous creation, a hand...its many bones, its thumb, how it works. But for such a hand to be the hand of the Son of God! Here he was, looking for all the world to be a child of Joseph. All those people knew it: "This is Joseph and Mary's son." He knew it, too. But he knew as well that he was for all the world the Son of God! For all the world! Did he find it astounding to be himself in the flesh? "What is a good God like me doing in a place like this?" If he did, if ever he thought like that about his overlay of flesh, might he also have concluded, "This flesh, my flesh, is given to me so that I can give it for the life of the world"?

Whatever he did, whatever he said, only some believed and followed. Others murmured. That being true in small Palestine, the ratio of those put off to those drawn would no doubt also be true throughout the world as the good news was spread. What would make the love of God in living flesh have even more drawing power? God's answer? God in flesh dying! There could be no greater proof of love than this, that God in flesh would lay down his life for his friends (John 15:13). God, abundant in grace, commended his love to us, while we were sinners, by having his anointed one die, die on a cross. Jesus said, "I, when I am lifted up from the earth, will draw all people unto me." God in flesh dying — how *attractive* even as it causes us to weep bitterly, how it draws us even though each detail grieves us. Could it be that our Lord thought in some way as the nails were driven into his hands, "This is my flesh, given to me that I can give it for the life of the world? This greater love I am showing to them, laying down my life to make them friends. My flesh...where the thorns pierce; my flesh...my back...my heart breaking at the ridicule, the rejection...my flesh given for the life of the world!"

Flesh must have seemed to his divine nature as something rather expendable, something taken on that could be given away without affecting his being. When Jesus thought of himself in the symbol of bread, something to be given to the hungry and eaten by them, perhaps it seemed but a further image to speak of his flesh as something to be given for the life of the world, as something to be eaten for the forgiveness he took on flesh to gain. No wonder he could say so simply and yet so profoundly, "Take and eat. This is my body given for you." He had been giving it all along.

I would not wish to try to one-up the scriptures, but there is one act of love that would seem to be greater than giving up one's life for one's friends. That would be arising out of that dying and raising up those friends to life eternal. He has done the dying. He has done his own rising. He will follow through with raising us up, now in our time of living and then after our time of dying. As our flesh wearies, as we draw nearer its fate of death, as we know loneliness in our world, in our homes, even in our families, we need not fear or doubt. Remember that he said of those drawn to him by his Father, "I will raise them up on the last day." He knows all the ills our flesh is heir to. He who gave his flesh into death for the life of the world is with us still, in the flesh, though we see him not. He invites us, as he invited his disciples, "Why are you frightened, and why do doubts arise in your hearts? Look at my hands and my feet; see that it is I myself. Touch me and see; for a ghost does not have flesh and bones as you see that I have" (Luke 24:38-39).

In the flesh, he is with us always. In the flesh, seen by faith, he gives himself still for the life of the world.

John 6:51-58   Proper 15
                                                    Pentecost 13
                                                 Ordinary Time 20

Himself The Real Presence

Accustomed as we are to hearing the words, "This is my body" in the consecration of the sacrament and "The body of Christ" as we receive holy communion bread, do we still draw back in surprise at hearing our Lord say "flesh"? Accustomed as we are to hearing the words "The blood of Christ" when we take the chalice, do we still find a murmur rising in our minds as we hear this text: "Unless you eat the flesh of the Son of Man and drink his blood, you have no life in you"?

The gospel for today seems very straightforward. Jesus, who had said to them, "I am the bread of life," rephrases his words slightly, saying, "I am the living bread that came down from heaven." Now he alters the promise that as the living bread he gives life to the world. He had earlier said, "Whoever *comes* to me, and whoever *believes* in me...they will never be hungry and never be thirsty." Now Jesus says, "Whoever *eats* of this bread will live forever." Up to this section of John's gospel's sixth chapter Jesus has used "bread" to refer to his teaching and his ministry. In the section given for today there is a change. He defines "bread" in a different way. "The bread that I will give for the life of the world is my flesh." And — it's true, isn't it? — that word "flesh" gives us pause.

It also stopped his hearers. It started a dispute. "How can this man give us his flesh to eat?" Jesus does not explain *how*. Instead he becomes even more specific: "Very truly, I tell you, unless you eat the flesh of the Son of Man and drink his blood, you have no life in you." Then he restates that in positive terms, "Those who eat my flesh and drink my blood have eternal life, and I will raise them up at the last day; for my flesh is true food and my blood is true drink." Even more, that gives us pause, doesn't it?

Interesting, isn't it, where we find the sticking point? We — most of us — do not cavil at the assertion, "I came down from heaven." Those first hearers did. But we don't — most of us. Nor do we tilt our heads in a questioning way at the direct statement, "I will raise them up on the last day." We — most of us — accept in faith, quite unquestioning faith, that the second person of the Holy Trinity, the Son, became incarnate, that is, that divine being "was made man" as the Creed states it. Not simply a man, a male child, a boy baby, although that we accept as true, but more than that, the representative of all human beings. In the Genesis account Adam was the first person, and at first the only person, the totality of all humankind. Then Adam and Eve were everybody in the world. When scriptures call Jesus the Second Adam, he stands for everybody in the world. He stands for all of us as representative. He died for all of us. He was raised from the dead as the first fruits of all of us who are dying and of all those who have died. He will raise up all the dead and give eternal life to all who believe.

Are you following this? We — most of us — accept all this in faith without a dubious murmur or complaint. And all this is — what shall we say? — "unbelievable" stuff. It is "unknowable." Only by divine revelation in scripture and only by inner working of the Holy Spirit, only by faith do we accept all this as true.

But we get stuck on "eat my flesh." We look for an alternative at "drink my blood." We understand that when Jesus said that he was "the bread of God which comes down from heaven and gives life to the world" he was using a figure of speech. He was *like* manna. He was *like* the basic staple of food that sustains life. And even though he did not mention any liquid or say that *he* was living water, we had no difficulty in accepting the claim Jesus was making that he was all that we need to have real life, here and forever. We would not be hungry and we would not be thirsty, that is, we would be fully satisfied if we accepted Jesus' claims, Jesus' word and work.

Now he goes beyond metaphor, beyond figures of speech. He says, "I am speaking of my *flesh*. I am referring to my *blood*. The flesh that developed in nine months in the womb of Mary. The blood that coursed through my veins and cheeks in the manger. The blood that colored the bandage Mary put on my finger when I cut it with Joseph's saw in the carpenter shop. Flesh and blood are mine, flesh-and-blood adds up to *me*. This is what I will give for the life of the world. I will give my flesh and blood on the cross like a lamb sacrificed, the lamb of God taking away the sins of the world. Flesh nailed on the cross. Flesh pierced by the spear. Blood from that side, from those hands, from the crown of thorns, from the scourge. Blood that cleanses from all sin. I am saying that my flesh now is also true food and my blood is true drink. I am saying that those who eat my flesh and drink my blood have eternal life." This is what we hear Jesus saying. Jesus said to the crowd after the feeding of the thousands, "This is the work of God, that you believe in him whom he has sent."

Not that this is simple. Interpreters differ on the meaning of the entire section. Some argue that the words "eating" and "drinking" are to be interpreted as figures of speech. Then the passage would only be urging hearers to assimilate for their own well-being all that Jesus was about to accomplish in his flesh and blood passion. Some think these were part of John's report of Christ's institution of the sacrament of Holy Communion which otherwise goes unreported in this gospel. In the sequence of John's account these events take place much before the Lord's last supper with his disciples. These hearers would not have been able to connect the Lord's words with the eating and drinking of that sacrament. Those scholars think these verses were placed here as the manuscripts were copied because of their similarity to Christ's description of himself as "bread." They hold, however, that these words of the Lord do describe in specific terms the eating and drinking which the Savior instituted in the sacrament of his last supper. And the Savior says, both here and in the accounts of the supper's institution, "my body and my blood."

For most of us who believe the incarnation of our Lord, who believe that he was conceived into flesh, these words really matter. They describe how that real presence of God *in matter* continues today. In the gift of flesh and blood his real presence in matter is discernible until he returns in visible presence.

It could help us to think this through under two headings. The first is the meal. The second is the menu.

Of all the human actions Jesus is described as doing, eating and drinking are perhaps the most familiar. Only suffering is more specifically detailed. He is never pictured as laughing. He wept only a few tears. The divine-human Jesus ate and drank as naturally and as necessarily as we all. When he wanted to assure his followers that he truly was alive after his dying, when he had returned to be with them, he asked, "Have you anything here to eat?" The disciples then gave him a piece of broiled fish, "and he took it and ate in their presence" (Luke 24:41-43). What was always "unnatural" or rather "supernatural" was that it was *God* sharing in the bread and wine, the fish and the vegetables. It was God fellowshipping with his friends in our warmest expression of unity — a meal. When, therefore, Jesus wanted a memorial to make sure his followers would always hold him in their minds, a way to continue his presence among them, he started a supper, with eating and drinking. He could, no doubt, have stayed on once he had risen from the dead and not ascended after the forty days. He could have made Jerusalem his headquarters and let pilgrimages develop as the way we could keep in touch with him. He could have instituted a ceremonial touching of his garment as the way to receive power from him. Instead he decided on a meal. (Of course, we are conjecturing — so Saint Paul once said — as fools.)

A meal, then. Yes. We can concede that. But the menu? Of course, we speak of this, too, as fools. It is not our business. But it may supply a way for our limited minds to think God-thoughts, to ponder what indeed our Lord did. The menu: "My flesh is true food and my blood is true drink," Jesus said. What was the divine strategy for our salvation? It hinged on putting flesh on God. God would appropriate our human nature and "be found in fashion as a man." Human nature consists of more than flesh and blood, of course. But for us who are *sensible*, who depend upon our five senses to understand, flesh and blood are the things which we can touch and see, the things by which we recognize humanity, the things that sum up for us living beings.

God, therefore, just as he gave us his Son in our human nature, and made him visible in flesh and blood, also decided to continue his divine presence among us by making the flesh and blood of the incarnate Son available to us — this time not only for us to see and to touch, but to eat and to drink. God continues to give us himself, to give us the same Beloved Son once given to us incarnate, to give us *him* in bread and wine, to give us his body and his blood in a meal. And so Jesus Christ continues to *be*, to be among us, God, filling all things, with us always, incarnate but invisible, making his presence known, making his blessings available to us in his body and blood with the gifts of bread and wine in this meal of remembrance.

Ours not to reason why this way, of course, but does not this attempt to understand help us as we hear Jesus say, "Very truly, I tell you, unless you eat the flesh of the Son of Man and drink his blood you have no life in you"? Does it not help us as we hear Jesus in this post-resurrection phrasing of his earlier words, "I am the way, and the truth, and the life. No one comes to the Father except through me" (John 14:6)? And all this is said positively in this gospel: "Those who eat my flesh and drink my blood abide in me, and I in them. Just as the living Father sent me, and I live because of the Father, so whoever eats me will live because of me."

We do not ask the "how can this man give us his flesh to eat" question, but we often do wonder *why*. Our Lord ate and drank with sinners while he was seen among us. We are sinners still. Will not his love prompt him to break bread with us as well? Since he has promised to be with us always, even though invisible, do we not rejoice at this promise, "Those who eat my flesh and drink my blood abide in me, and I in them"? How greatly blessed, we, who eat and drink with him, who eat and drink — *him*!

John 6:56-69 (C)   Proper 16
John 6:60-69 (RC)   Pentecost 14
                               Ordinary Time 21

The Final Questions

We are all being taught by God. Jesus cited that in one of the lessons from John's gospel we have heard on the last four Sundays. We have been taught. We have learned. Today we have the final exam. The gospel poses a number of questions. They seem to be rhetorical, asked simply for effect. No answer seems to be expected. But how successful would a student be who, seeing his final examination, looks up and says to the instructor, "I assume all these questions are rhetorical"?

Are you ready? Give answers to the following questions. The first is raised by some in the crowd of followers around Jesus. They may have been among those who, like us, have been with Jesus since he first distributed the bread and fish to the thousands. With them we have learned that Jesus is the prophet greater than Moses. With them, we have heard Jesus tell us that he is a great deal more significant than the manna of Moses as well. He is "the bread of God which comes down from heaven and gives life to the world." The third thing we have learned along with them is that Jesus is God in the flesh giving himself for the world. The last lesson taught to us last Sunday was this: Jesus Christ gives us his flesh and blood to eat and to drink in the Sacrament. By this gift he abides in us and we in him.

These were the lessons which prompted the first question. Some in the class said, "This teaching is difficult; who can accept it?" Rhetorical, of course. Or it could have been their way of saying, "We certainly can't accept it." In any case the question is ours to answer. "Who can accept his teaching?" Answer: "We can. We can accept it." This is no true or false exam. Explain your answer. How can you? How can you believe such claims by this man? He is the son of Mary. His father is Joseph the carpenter. How can you, why do you, accept Jesus as the Son of God? How can you believe that he came from heaven to be friend and savior?

It is amazing, isn't it? Amazing that we believe what he taught. You have heard people say, "I wish I could have a faith like yours. I wish I could be as sure as you seem to be that there is a God who cares, a God who will see one through evil and trouble, who promises a happy life after death."

We're all in this exam together. We can talk to each other during the test. Most of us began to believe when we were infants. Before we knew it, we believed. Before we could understand the questions, we knew the answers. Baptism's water is a washing of rebirth. We were indeed born anew at our baptizing, born as children of God, accepted by God and accepting God and all God's works and ways. More than that. What God's Spirit began with water, the Spirit continued with words. We learned from parents, pastors, teachers, all these difficult-to-believe things, and the Spirit sealed our faith by hearing. Enough on question one. Who can accept it? We can, because as Jesus says here, "The words that I have spoken to you are spirit and life."

The second question comes from the Lord: "Does this offend you?" He is asking us about all that he has been claiming about himself. Phillips phrases the question: "Is this too much for you?" Raymond Brown translates it, "Does it shake your faith?" Many of us can answer quickly, "No," and be ready to go on to the next question. But this is indeed a difficult one. Some of you on the fringe of the Church, some even in the center pews, will admit that you find much of this difficult to accept. No doubt Jesus must say of this crowd as he did of that one, "Among you are some who do not believe." Jesus knew Judas and yet called him to be a disciple.

He calls each one of us. And he can be very persuasive. Think again of what he tells of himself. "I am God, with the Father and the Holy Spirit, the divine Trinity. I was born of the virgin Mary by a miraculous overshadowing by the Spirit. I grew up as a boy and then a man, but I was always also the Son of God. Is this too much for you?"

Jesus asks another question to help you rise above your doubts: "What if you were to see the Son of Man ascending to where he was before?" What do we say? Perhaps it helped them to see Jesus suddenly be lifted up out of their sight, to see him disappear into a cloud. But we have only read the report. That's one of the difficult things to believe, all this "up" and "down" talk. Is that reasonable for our scientific age?

Is it too much for you? Then answer, "Yes." That is not a wrong answer. It throws you now. So? We must all be taught of God. Stay in God's school. Hear Jesus remind you, "For this reason I have told you that no one can come to me unless it is granted by the Father." We whose faith is *not* shaken can assure you that God does want you to be able to grasp all this. God certainly put himself out in sending the Son to earth. God will surely not want all that effort to be wasted. If God did it, God surely will want us to know he did it. The Spirit is God's follow-through. The Spirit is even now teaching you by this word. "It is the Spirit that gives life," Jesus says in this text, "the flesh is useless." That is our Lord's way of urging you to realize God knows the answers. Use your head and don't exaggerate your brains. Realize your common sense would obviously not apply to God's uncommonly divine wisdom and God's one-of-a-kind action.

Now to the rest of us, to us who count ourselves among the believing disciples. The next question is, "Do you also wish to go away?" Don't answer too quickly. It's not so simple. Many who once were followers have indeed left off this following. Jesus asks, "Do you also wish to go away?" Think about it as asking you, "Will you? Will you, too, go away?"

It is a potentially frightening fact that while only the heavenly Father can draw us, every one of us can *with*draw. Go away. After one of the twelve betrayed him, all the remaining eleven fled. It is an equally comforting fact that all eleven were drawn back and were thereafter faithful unto death. Of course, most of them were martyred. If the question is phrased, "Will you also go away?" we would have to answer, "Yes and no." Out of sad experience, we realize we have gone away. And out of confident trust we say, "Though all others become deserters...I will never desert you" (Matthew 26:43). Hear the cock crow? That is exactly what Peter said. At best we can be only cautiously confident about ourselves. But we can be confident about God, and we can say in the words of Philippians 1:6: "I am confident of this, that the one who began a good work [in me] will bring it to completion by the day of Jesus Christ."

"Do you wish to go away?" We answer that question with a firm, "No! I do not wish to go away." Now, quote it to yourself: "If wishes were horses, then beggars would ride." Get on your horse and faithfully "continue in his word," continue in "the apostles' teaching and fellowship" and "in breaking of bread and the prayers" (Acts 2:42). The issue here is really what this exam was all about. Some no longer went about with him because they said the teaching of Jesus was difficult. We who do not wish to go away take the opposite approach. *Because* what our Lord expects is difficult, *therefore* we will stay close; we will always go about with him. We will receive him as he gives himself to us. He will abide in us and we will abide in him.

Now the final exam's final question. Simon Peter asked it after the Lord's query, "Do you also wish to go away?" He asked, "Lord, to whom can we go?" Would we be shocked if we heard the Lord interrupt and say, "You can go to hell"? But that alternative is right there in John 3:16: "perish," remember? God loved the world so that not everyone would perish, not be lost. That's not the answer we want to hear or to give. Try some other "go" phrases. "Let us now go even unto Bethlehem and see what has taken place." The shepherds were wise men. And so was Simon Peter and so were all these disciples. They were "wise unto salvation." They could say, "We have come; we have come to believe and to know that you are the Holy One of God. You have the words of eternal life."

Where can we go? Try another.

> *Go to dark Gethsemane ...*
> *Follow to the judgment hall ...*
> *Calvary's mournful mountain climb ...*

But don't stop there. Go to Joseph's garden.

> *Early hasten to the tomb ...*
> *Christ is ris'n! He meets our eyes.*
> *Savior, teach us so to rise.*
> ("Go To Dark Gethsemane," James Montgomery)

Then the truly final stanza, to pass the test with flying colors!

> *When we on that final journey go*
> *That Christ is for us preparing,*
> *We'll gather in song, our hearts aglow,*
> *All joy of the heavens sharing.*
> *And walk in the light of God's own place,*
> *With angels his name adoring.*
> ("O Day Full Of Grace," N.F.S. Grundtvig)

Mark 7:1-8, 14-15, 21-23

Proper 17
Pentecost 15
Ordinary Time 22

Our Dilemma And Delight

For the past five Sundays the lectionary has assigned gospels from John. Now the lectionary takes us back to Mark. Five Sundays have stressed divine perfection. This Sunday points up our human imperfection. But a "perfection/imperfection" contrast does not quite express the intense difference which is illustrated between the divine and the human. The Sunday gospels from John were about the irruption of the divine into this world. Today's gospel is about the corruption of humans in the world. Sick at heart, that is the way our Lord describes us. "It is from within, from the human heart, that evil intentions come." All of us have come apart at the heart, apart from God. Jesus cites the passage from Isaiah: "This people honors me with their lips, but their hearts are far from me."

The thrust of this Sunday's teaching, however, is not condemning; it is not critical. Rather it is challenging. It does not so much tell us again what we can't do, but it urges us to realize what we can do. James urges us: "Rid yourselves of all sordidness and rank growth of wickedness" (James 1:21). Weeds there are, rank weeds; but we can weed our own patch. In a well-known passage from Ephesians we are told: "Be strong in the Lord ... Take up the whole armor of God so that you may be able to withstand ... to stand firm." We are engaged in "war without" and against "foes within." Within are "enemies of blood and flesh." The war without is against "the wiles of the devil." Reasons enough to put on "the whole armor of God." And back of it all, back of us, is the power of God which will enable us to be sure that we can, indeed, stand firm.

Focus first on the foes within. The heart of our danger is that we tend to be in favor of our foes. That is the significance of the phrases Jesus utters: "Their hearts are far from me" and "Evil intentions come from within, from the human heart." The word "heart" connotes the center of our reason, of our will. What we want, what we desire, what we wish for, these things originate at the center of our existence; they reveal what we are really like at the center of our being. And the heart's desire becomes the hands' deeds: "Fornication, theft, murder, adultery, avarice, wickedness, deceit, licentiousness, envy, slander, pride, folly — all these evil things come from within, and they defile a person."

However, we are not only in favor of our foes — we also fight them. We *don't* want to do these things that we must confess we *do* want to do. As confusing as that is, as much as that reveals about our split personalities, it is tremendously good news. What is good about it is that it reveals how close God has deliberately come to our human hearts that are far from him. Paul described our dilemma and our delight in his own case like this: "I am of the flesh, sold into slavery under sin. I do not understand my own action. For I do not do what I want, but I do the very thing that I hate." Our dilemma. Now our delight. "I delight in the law of God in my inmost self ... Thanks be to God through Jesus Christ our Lord!" (Romans 7:14-25). Our dilemma — a heart in us defiled. Our delight — a heart devoted to God who has rescued us.

Think again of how the dilemma of our evil desiring has been bracketed by our delight in the law of God. We can't think of what God has done for us as a heart transplant. Like a person who has had a heart attack, we live on with a permanently damaged center of our will. How can we describe what God has done for us through Jesus Christ our Lord? God performed *his own* divine heart transplant. God conceived a human heart into *himself,* into the divine Being, when the Son of God was conceived by the Holy Spirit in the womb of the virgin Mary. But as much like us as Jesus was when he was born, when he grew up, even when he died, he was completely different at the heart of his matter, at the center of his being. He was without sin. He had no heart problem. He was God's delight, with none of sinful humanity's dilemma.

What could God in Christ do then to make us different? Think of us as realistically, as physically, as Jesus described us. In words which the lectionary skips, he speaks of what we eat going into our stomachs and out into the sewer. Equally blunt language can best describe our inner defilement. We were defiled in the very gut of our being. With such a diagnosis of our sick selves, what would be the prescription for our cure? If we could only turn ourselves inside out, if only all our defilement within could be flushed out, if our sin could be removed and we be given a new "delight in the law of God in our inmost self," if only the prayer could be answered, "Create in me a clean heart, O God, and renew a right spirit within me."

Behold the Man! "Ecce Homo." Pilate's words point us to God's solution. Jesus was whole man, was holy as man. And Jesus opened himself up completely. He fully revealed his inmost being to us. He turned himself inside out for us. By what he did as by what he said, he revealed to us what life should be like, revealed to us the perfect life. But more than that. A "model of the godly life," an example of perfect living by itself would only underscore our dilemma and drive us to despair. God's solution was that the Savior would also be "a sacrifice for sin." We can not adequately explain to ourselves how a perfect life and an undeserved death could take the place of our millions of imperfect lives and deserved deaths. God is the one owed, and God has agreed to the coin. To replace our inner defilement, our Savior turned his nature inside out for us. He made himself to be sin for us, though he had no sin. Then God-in-Christ let all the inner evil of humanity happen to him. The sins he warned us against were turned against him. "The things that come out are what defile," he said. Those sins came out of those who rose up against Jesus. They did not defile him, they did not destroy him, they did not deter him, but they terribly damaged him, they caused his death. Number them, name them, and remember how they struck mortal blows against him. The folly! "You killed the prince of life!" The pride! "Prophesy to us! Hail, King of the Jews!" The slander: "We found this man perverting our nation."

The envy: even Pilate realized that "it was out of jealousy that the chief priests had handed him over." The licentiousness! They accused him, "This man is a glutton and a wine bibber." The deceit: "Why do we still need witnesses? You have heard his blasphemy!" The wickedness, the avarice, the adultery, the fornication, the theft — all the sins of all the world of all the ages — he took the death wage of our sins upon himself. The murder: Pilate said to them, "What do you wish me to do with the man you call the King of the Jews?" They shouted back, "Crucify him!" Then the Roman soldiers took him to Golgatha, and they crucified him.

Then, of course, the resurrection! No! Not "of course." He, this Jesus, fought to the death "the rulers, the authorities, the cosmic power of this present darkness, against the spiritual forces of evil in the heavenly places" and he "quenched all the flaming arrows of the evil one" (Ephesians 6:12-16). What seemed at first to his despairing disciples to be a Pyrrhic victory, one that took the Lord's life as he tried to save our lives, turned out to be a cosmic victory. God re-created his own world. His was the ultimate "generous act of giving." This perfect gift of forgiven life was given to us "from above, coming down from the Father of lights." Nor was it an abstract gift existing as some sort of accounting ploy, some use of double accounting books. No — it was a gift given to each of us. "He gave us birth by the word of truth so that we would become a kind of first fruits of his creatures" (James 1:17-18).

It was God's way of solving our dilemma. Our hearts were far from him. In Christ Jesus God came very near to us. We are near to the heart of God. God raised Jesus from the dead, his glorified heart began beating again, and he drew near to us anew. He remains with us always. We are in Christ. Christ abides in us. His heart is so close even our feeble hearts are no longer far from God. For the giant foes that remain for us to fight, he equips us with "the whole armor of God" — and it fits! We can fight the good fight, fight in the "war without" and against the "foes within."

With high delight
Let us unite
In songs of sweet jubilation.

You pure in heart,
Each take your part,
Sing Jesus Christ,
Our salvation!
    ("With High Delight Let Us Unite" by Georg Vetter)

Nor has God failed to provision his armed followers. God knows his army travels on heavenly food.

Mark 7:24-37 (C)
Mark 7: 31-37 (RC)

Proper 18
Pentecost 16
Ordinary Time 23

Cheers For The Healed

Let's Hear It For The Deaf Man — that's the title of a detective novel. That could mean, "Do his listening for him." But, for today, let it mean, "Three cheers for the deaf man." The deaf man deserves our first cheers, but before we give him his desserts, let's hear the voice of this Sunday telling us to cheer for some others as well. "Let's hear it for those who have heard and for those who now hear the word of the Lord." Another group deserves cheers: "Let's hear it for those whose tongues are released and who speak plainly, who proclaim the love of the Lord." Another group: "Let's hear it for those who have seen, for those who see, the salvation of the Lord." And finally: "Let's hear it for those who once were lame, those who now leap like the deer, those who have become eager doers of the word."

These are groups which today's lessons single out for praise. We are all members of these groups. The point of all this is that in Christ Jesus we are new creatures. What we have become by God's grace is something to cheer about. The Word has changed us.

Think about the changed life of this man who had been deaf. He was transformed by, literally, a word: *Ephphatha*, a double word in English: "Be opened." Actually his whole life was changed by the Word-made-flesh. He was changed by the Son of God who had emptied himself, had turned his divinity inside out and become an earthly pedestrian, like us, who was walking from the region of

Tyre, going by way of Sidon toward the Sea of Galilee, in the region of the Decapolis. He just happened — so it might seem — to be near this deaf man, and he healed him with a word. What a happening! But it was nothing compared to that happy day when God the Son was born for us, lived for us, died for us. What happened to Jesus after that death has also happened to us, in our different situation, of course. He was resurrected. We have been regenerated. By his word in the water of baptism, with his word, we have been given new life. By the word which is continually being spoken to us our ears have been opened, and we have heard, we hear. By his speaking to our hearing we are strengthened and sanctified. God has opened our ears to hear. Let's hear it for all who have heard the word of the Lord!

It is not our hearing alone that has been changed. Our entire being has been transformed. The old nature has been forgiven. The new nature has been created. In his first chapter, James spells it out: "In the fulfillment of his own purpose [the Father of lights] gave us birth by the word of truth, so that we would become a kind of first fruits of his creatures" (James 1:18). The heart, the center of our being, that was the source of things wicked, has been overlaid with a new heart, a clean heart. We have been renewed by God's free Spirit. The mind that was left after the fall, the mind that refused to mind God's law, the mind that mocked God's word and boasted, "Your thoughts are not my thoughts," has been paralleled by a right mind. Now we have the mind of Christ. We live, and yet it is not the old "we" but it is now Christ who lives in us. Let's hear it for the new creature! Let's hear all this as the new creatures we are, and let's cheer our renewed selves.

G. K. Chesterton in his autobiography wrote about the effect of forgiveness, of the absolution. He was referring to the words of absolution spoken by the presiding minister after a confession of sin: "I forgive you all your sins in the name of the Father and of the Son and of the Holy Spirit." Somewhat freely paraphrased, this is what Chesterton said: Forgiven Christians "do truly, by definition, step out again into that dawn of their own beginning ... God has really remade them in his own image. They are now, each one of them, a new experiment as they were when they were really only five years old. They stand in the white light at the worthy beginning of a new life. The accumulations of time [of previous sinning] can no longer terrify. They may be grey and gouty; but they are only five minutes old."[1]

That is what we are. Phillips translates Paul: "Don't you realize that you yourselves are the temple of God, and that God's Spirit lives in you? ... His temple is holy — *and that is exactly what you are!*" (1 Corinthians 3:16-17). Let's hear it for us all, for us who have heard, who hear the word of the Lord.

The man once deaf was also mute. But Jesus did everything well. He enabled this man to hear unheard of things and this speechless man to proclaim the word of the Lord. Let's hear it for those whose tongues proclaim the love of the Lord. This man's tongue was loosed as his ears were opened "and he spoke plainly." "Jesus ordered them to tell no one." The word he wanted spread was that God had come to redeem his people, not that there was a faith healer in the Decapolis. "But the more he ordered them, the more zealously they proclaimed it." We have been ordered — more than they were ordered not to — we have been ordered to proclaim the word of the Lord, to tell the love of God for the world. "Say to those who are of a fearful heart," says Isaiah, "be strong, do not fear! You who were deaf have had your ears unstopped. You whose tongues were speechless can now sing for joy." Today's message instructs us to do what we *can* do. We can sing for joy, and not merely because we have much to be glad about, but in order to let others hear the good news that they, too, can be glad. Our tongues have been loosed, not for loose talk, but for the words that free. James cautions us about thoughtless talk: "You must understand this, my beloved: let everyone be quick to listen, slow to speak ... " (James 1:19); that is, slow to speak in anger. We could add, slow just to chit chat, to simply pass the time of day, to share the latest news.

Doctors can see that something is wrong with us when they have us stick out our tongues and say, "Ah." God can sadly tell what is wrong with us when what we say reveals selfishness or partiality. James warns against saying to the ones with gold rings and fair clothes, "Have a seat here, please," while we mutter to the poor, "Stand there," or "Sit at my feet" (James 2:2-3). We are not to make free with our freedom of speech. "If any think they are religious, and do not bridle their tongues but deceive their hearts, their religion is worthless" (James 1:26). What is our religion, our joy, worth? What these people did against orders we are to do as ordered: "zealously proclaim" the good news that the God and Father of our Lord Jesus Christ has enabled us to sing for joy. Let's hear it for him who has loved us, who has released us from our bonds. Let's hear it for those who proclaim the love of the Lord.

This man, who had ears made for hearing, Jesus enabled to hear. To us, who have eyes to see, God has said, "Behold!" Let's hear it for those who have seen, for all of us who see, the works of the Lord, the salvation of our God. Isaiah again: "Then the eyes of the blind shall be opened" (Isaiah 35:5). Look at yourself in the mirror to which James refers. He wrote that people who are merely hearers of the word and not doers are like people who see their image in a mirror but do not really realize what they are like. With any degree of honesty, we see ourselves as we have proved ourselves to be — and there is little beauty that we should pride ourselves. But do we really realize what we have become, what changed persons God has made us to be? Look in the mirror of all the word and works of the Lord given you for years and years. Do you, "going away, immediately forget what you are like"? What you are like! You are now made likeable. God is love, making you lovable, lovely. When you see yourself as the holy Other sees you, do you, are you, seeing that you are freed, that you are now under the perfect law, the law of liberty? In many ways the blind must have others lead them. You *see*! You see yourself! You yourself see!

Of course, you did not see this deaf man healed. But you are even more blessed because the Spirit has given you faith and understanding from what these first Christians saw. And this healing that announced the fulfillment of Isaiah's prophecy was only a part of the beginning of the salvation of our God. They saw, and we believe, the ending. The Lord, hanging on the cross, closing his eyes in death as a ransom for us all, that seemed like the ending. Let's hear it for the Lamb of God sacrificed for the sin of the world! But the surprise ending is the guarantee of our salvation. On the third day God raised him from the dead, raised him for our salvation, raised him so that we might be alive in Christ Jesus. Let's hear it for the risen Lord! Let's hear it for all those who have seen by faith the salvation of our God!

One more. Isaiah prophesied that when God would come to save us, "then the lame shall leap like a deer" (Isaiah 35:6). Let's hear it for those who hop to it to be doers of the word. James admonishes: "Be doers of the word, and not merely hearers, who deceive themselves ... The doers who act, they will be blessed in their doing" (James 1:22, 25). We might well wonder what this man did after he could hear and speak. People might have thought of all this after Peter and John healed a man who had been lame from his birth. Peter took him by the hand and raised him up. "Jumping up, he stood and began to walk, and he entered the temple with them, walking and leaping and praising God" (Acts 3:7-8). Let's hear it for the walking, leaping, praising healed lame man. It is, perhaps, a smaller miracle when we manage to bridle our tongues, when we push aside self-centeredness and "care for orphans and widows in their distress," when we remember who we are, whose we are, and "keep ourselves unstained by the world" (James 1:27).

Let's hear it for us, hearers, proclaimers, beholders, doers!

The crowd said about Jesus, "He has done everything well." Our Lord says of us, "With you I have done fairly well, if I do say so myself." When the day of the Lord comes, when we see him as he is, when we hear him welcome us, when we come walking and leaping and praising God to the table spread with the feast to come, may it be said of us, may the Lord say to us, "Well done, good and faithful servants! You have done everything well, hearing and telling, seeing and doing! Enter into the joy of your Lord!"

Let's hear that!

---

1. Cited in *For All the Saints*, Frederick J. Schumacher, editor (Delhi, New York: American Lutheran Publicity Bureau, 1994), p. 48. From *Autobiography*. Copyright by A. P. Witt, Ltd., 1936, copyright renewed.

Mark 8:27-38 (C)
Mark 8:27-35 (RC)

Proper 19
Pentecost 17
Ordinary Time 24

The Taught Can

You have heard that it has been said in old times, "Those who can, do; those who can't, teach." But I say unto you this morning, "Those who are taught, can do." As one who has been taught, I say this unto you as to those who have been taught by God, "Having been taught, we *can*."

All this is pertinent to us all because as the Preacher in Ecclesiastes wrote, "For everything there is a season, and a time for every matter under heaven" (Ecclesiastes 3:1). Are we aware of what time it is? There is a time to be taught and a time to do.

Quite clearly for the disciples this was a time to be taught. Mark relates the call of some of the first disciples early in his book. He tells of the appointment of the twelve as apostles and tells of how Jesus sent them out two by two on a mission. But it is quite clear that Jesus regarded these days chiefly as classroom days.

All the world's population was to become his pupils, but for the time of his ministry on earth he limited his lectures to Palestine. He focused much of his instruction on the twelve. Small group discussion was in his lesson plan. On this morning the instruction began with what was designed to be a discussion question. "Who do people say that I am?" One couldn't miss on that question. There could be no wrong answer. But it led up to the real issue: "Who do *you* say that I am?" Peter, as always, had his hand up. Did some of the others have that thwarted feeling? "You always call on Peter. I had my hand up first." They had all learned the correct answer: "You are the Messiah." Whether they understood the definition of "Messiah" any better than Peter did is rather doubtful.

It was still the time for being taught. Jesus did not want them going off proclaiming some half-truths. "He strongly ordered them not to tell anyone about him." As he continued to teach them, he spelled out how "the Son of Man must undergo great suffering, and be rejected by the elders, the chief priests, and the scribes and be killed, and after three days rise again." Then Peter again — and Peter's attitude makes clear why Jesus was not yet ready to let them go out witnessing. Jesus had told them these details "quite openly." Peter took Jesus aside. Was he thinking that he ought not embarrass Jesus before the others? Still, someone had to set him straight. Peter rebuked him. "You've got it all wrong, Jesus. With what you've got, you can take over as Messiah easily. You don't have to take second place to these scribes and priests and elders."

Clearly the problem was in the definition of terms. "Messiah" for Peter seemed to mean some sort of political leader who would restore the kingdom to Israel. Messiahship could be achieved by a popularity ploy which would make his fame pay off, which would perhaps get people to declare him king.

We think of Jesus as a "can do" person, but clearly here he was first of all a "can teach" rabbi. His words are stern. They are rebuke. They are designed to set Peter and the disciples straight, to get them in line — and that line was behind him, lined up in support of him, following his lead, following him. Jesus wanted more than that the disciples would mouth the right answers, agree with him with or without understanding. He wanted disciples, followers, individuals who could and would not only follow after him but who would take over after him, would take the lead after his visible presence was taken from the earth. His teaching was aimed at his disciples's doing. What he said was, "Get behind me, Satan! For you are setting your mind not on divine things but on human things."

The text tells us that Jesus turned from the twelve and addressed the crowd as well. But one could well imagine that before that he first reviewed his basic instruction with the twelve. Whether Jesus did that or not, it may be well for us to review who Jesus is and what he did, check our teaching before we consider our doing. "Now," we can imagine Jesus saying, "let's get this concept of Messiah straight." This is the lesson *we* have learned about what God-in-Christ was doing in a place like our world, then and now. We are mired in it, in the disaster and the distortion of what has become of that creation God once called very good. God does not want any of us to perish. He wants all of us to come to the knowledge of the truth.

The first part of God's truth is the mess we have made of our world and our lives. No one can be blind to the desecration of the planet. No one can avoid the wickedness that kills and maims, impoverishes and starves people in every country and city. Each of us must acknowledge personal enmities and selfishness and deliberate misdeeds. It is bad enough to realize how self-centered we are; it is even worse to comprehend the greater stupidity it is on our part to think we can dethrone God from life's real center. People sometimes apologize for evil or for bitter words: "I shouldn't have said that." But the tongue is only the messenger. The whole head is sick. The heart is apart from God. That is the truth, the first part of God's truth.

The second part of the truth was right there with the disciples and the crowd. It was he, Jesus. He is the truth, clear evidence that God loves his creation and, though he detests the world's evil, stands ready to take it. God was in Christ taking it, taking the awful results of evil into his own being. Then, in giving his life, he took sin's punishment of death away from us and suffered it himself.

We have learned what Jesus taught. We wouldn't dream of rebuking Jesus, or God the Father, for that matter, for the way God went about reconciling the world to himself. Who would argue with that success? We believe and are sure that Christ's suffering succeeded in saving us. Isaiah has words which can apply to our Lord as our teaching savior. Jesus had the tongue of a teacher, all right, with words that sustain the weary. God has "wakened our ears to listen as those who are taught." Though his soul was exceeding sorrowful as death impended, he was not rebellious. He did not turn backward. He gave his back to those who struck him and his cheeks to those who pulled out the beard. He did not hide his face from insult and spitting. He set his face like flint to obey in all things what the Father asked him to do. And he was not disgraced, not put to shame. God vindicated him before all enemies, before all doubters, before us. God who had him die for the sins that condemned us, raised him to life again as undebatable proof that evil and devil were defeated. Do we quarrel with that? We do not! We believe and we are sure that this Jesus is the Son of the living God, the living Son, our Living Savior (Isaiah 50:4f).

But what about our *doing*? Are we able to? Can we? Jesus took up the matter of deeds. "If any want to be my followers," he began. There is a time for faith and a time for works. James minces no words and makes mincemeat out of our excuses: "What good is it, my brothers and sisters, if you say you have faith but do not have works? Can faith save you? ... Faith by itself, if it has no works, is dead" (James 2:14-17). Well, we don't need James to make us feel guilty. We can do that for ourselves. But can we do more than that?

What was the first thing Jesus said we must do if we wish to be followers? "If any want to become my followers, let them deny themselves and take up their cross and follow me." Deny your *self* ... when we repent and believe the good news that already means we are denying ourselves. Do any of you claim that God owes you eternal living? Or do any of you claim that you can sin in order that grace may abound? Or do you do everything your foolish heart desires? Sometimes you do some of those things, but even then you deny yourself: "It is not I that do them, but sin that dwells in me." Of course, we pass the test of "let them deny themselves." We are not hearers only.

As for "taking up your cross," which is the follow-through Jesus expects, you're doing that, too. Sometimes, like Simon of Cyrene, we bear a cross that others force upon us. We may wish we did not have to, but we carry on. We, too, pray, "Nevertheless, not my will but thine be done." We cross out line items in our budgets so that there will be a share for God at the bottom line. It's true as well about our time — instead of having all our time on our hands, we offer some of it to God and we spend time for God's people. We may often groan and travail, but we get good things done, and, what's more, we're glad we do them; we rejoice that we have brought forth good works into the world.

Don't minimize your good works. So Abraham did more? So Abraham, the father of the faithful, seems to have done better than we of little faith? When he saw the three men standing by his tent pitched by the oak of Mamre, he ran to them and begged them to stay with him and rest. He had Sarah make flour cakes and served them with curds and milk and roast veal (Genesis 18:1-8). And you don't even look at the panhandler you pass by on a street downtown, and you teach your teenage drivers not to pick up hitchhikers — so what? This age, our non-civilization, our doped and violent dropouts demand different methods. And we use them. We set up shelters and call them Good Samaritan houses; we invite the hungry to sit at tables in places we call "Loaves and Fishes." And we invest heavy money for clothing the poor. That is much more than saying merely, "Keep warm and eat your fill," while doing nothing to supply bodily needs. Speaking of taking up your cross, you also fill out your income tax forms, and you vote for and help pay for governmental programs for the poor and needy. Eat your heart out, Abraham. Rejoice and be glad, all you. Lift up your heads!! Your redemption is showing through!

Nor ought we minimize what we are doing in this very hour. There is a time for doing these other "goods" and there is a time for doing good liturgy. God is not ashamed to be our God, and we are not ashamed to claim God as our God and to worship as part of our duty "him only to serve." Sunday after Sunday — doing your good liturgy! It does the whole body good! When you give to God the glory due his name, there is a feedback of blessing that comes from God to you, and encouragement that flows from these other saints to you. Yes, we come for the assurance of forgiveness — the better to be saints. Yes, we pray for life — the better to live with and for others. Yes, we seek salvation — the better to share it with others. We stop by church on the way to work. We come for teaching, because having been taught, we can!

Sometimes after a great thanksgiving meal, all you want to do is take a nap. Here now is this great meal, this Eucharist, this feast of thanksgiving. God gives us forgiveness, life and salvation with the bread that is our Lord's body, the wine that is our Lord's blood. Sometimes, it is true, in the days after this thanksgiving we are caught napping. But much of the time, most of the times, we go in the strength of this heavenly food forty days and forty nights. That's biblical talk for as long as necessary. And that is only as long as it takes until our next liturgy.

All things are ready. Lord, make us more ready and willing and able!

Mark 9:30-37

Proper 20
Pentecost 18
Ordinary Time 25

Last But Yet First

In order to be last, you must give others a place in front of you. This is important to realize if you are interested in reaching first place. For Jesus here says, "Whoever wants to be first must be last of all and servant of all." Realize also that, given the kind of world we are part of, the people whom you must permit to go before you will be a mixed bag, indeed. You can't pick and choose, because that would mean the discards would be behind you. They would become last. They would really be taking the place you want, because, since you want to be first, you must be last of all and servant of all. If you put people back, behind you, it might seem that you are getting close to being first, but actually you would have fallen back, you would no longer be close to being first. That is what Jesus said.

Jesus said this "first must be last in order to be first" word after the disciples failed to grasp that that was exactly what Jesus was about to do himself. He was about to permit a disciple to betray him, about to consent to being put to death, all this to make it possible for all people to be first with God.

The easy way out of this dilemma might seem to be to stop wanting to be first. Would that we could. By ourselves we can't. But God has already changed us and our wants so that what we really want is it be first with God. But that does not mean we can simply sit tight and let it happen. God supplies our "wants" and now expects us to exercise them. Something we *do* is required. We are to welcome the child, welcome the least of the Lord's siblings, say to those around us, "Come up higher, higher than you are, higher, perhaps, than you think you deserve to be, higher than me." It's not easy being last. It's even more difficult to stand aside for others to go before you, and to welcome those whose servants you are to be.

Think of a long line at the checkout counter at your grocery store. As you stand, last in line, you see a frail grandmother type carrying a basket with only two items, ready to take her place in line behind you, your cart filled with a dozen or more packages. No problem. "Do go ahead. You will be checked through before I'm unpacked." But then along comes another, this time a pushy type breezily saying, "Mind if I go ahead? I'm in sort of a hurry." Then — don't we all? — you want nothing better than to let that shopper earn the title of "greatest" by being stuck at the back of the line.

That's not a completely fair example, of course. There is such a thing as fairness and taking turns, egalitarianism and democracy, and all that. But think of the greatest of all greatness, what God has done for us. Here Jesus spells out again for his disciples what he is about to undertake in order to let us go first. All of us pushy types ... Some of us putting on meek masks of grand-motherliness ... All of us wearing out our welcome day after day ... And yet, always being welcomed again. Only the mind and the mercy of God can compute how it works — the Son of Man is betrayed into human hands — inhuman hands, we would like to say. He is killed on a cross. Three days after he is killed, he rises again; he is alive. The result of his passionate service is that every one of us prodigals is welcomed home again, is met by God the Father even while we are a great way off, a God and Father who calls us daughter and son and urges all the heavenly host to rejoice with him "for these my sons and daughters were lost but now they are found, they were dead in trespasses and sins, but now they are alive in Christ Jesus and by the Holy Spirit."

In one of Ngaio Marsh's novels of New Zealand, a *tiki*, a Maori religious symbol, has been given as a birthday gift to the leading lady of a group of actors from England. It is being passed from hand to hand through the company. They all find the figure grotesque and its fertility symbolism embarrassing. There is mocking laughter and muttered comments as the actors point out its strange features to one another. Inspector Roderick Alleyn is a bit ashamed for them and apologizes to a Maori doctor who is dining with them and has explained the figure's significance. "Oh," the doctor replies, pleasantly, "so my great-grandparents have laughed over the first crucifix they saw."[1] Surely we do not give our Lord cause to be ashamed of us? Christ crucified — "a stumbling block to Jews and foolishness to Gentiles," but surely not to us, "those who are the called." To us the crucified One is "Christ, the power of God and the wisdom of God" (1 Corinthians 1:23-25). The wisdom of God — even though the disciples "did not understand what he was saying and were afraid to ask him," surely we understand what he was talking about. "Odd of God" indeed, himself so to humble himself in Jesus, the Son, so as to be last and the servant of all, in order that he might be both under the law and nailed on the cross for us, and so that we might be welcomed by him into the family. Oh blessed oddness! What prodigals would reject the Father's welcome, the rings on their fingers, the festive robes on their shoulders; would complain about the way the Father formulated the welcome? And if we gladly accept this wisdom of God by which we are saved, will we not also agree to and understand this wise counsel to make ourselves last and make others welcome?

Now, of course, the issue is about passing that welcome along. Welcomed in that uninhibited, unlimited, unreserved, incomprehensible way, we are to welcome everyone whom God welcomes. Any friend of God's is to be a friend of ours. We are to choose to be the last of all and the servant of all. "Jesus took a little child and put it among them; and taking it in his arms, he said to them, 'Whoever welcomes one such child in my name welcomes me, and whoever welcomes me welcomes not me but the one who sent me.' " Moreover, there should be no stupid excuses that sound like Pilate as he washed his hands of Jesus. "Father, I am one who has sinned against heaven and against you, and am not therefore able to welcome just anyone. I will, therefore, ignore some and let them alone. I will welcome whom I like, only the ones I like, and let the rest go." Would we want God to hear further echoes of Pilate's speech: "I find no fault in those others. It's not that. I just don't like them. They're not my type. I will therefore chastise them and let them go."

What is our unwelcoming problem? In the Second Lesson, James makes our weakness very clear. "Where there is envy and selfish ambition, there will also be disorder and wickedness of every kind." James asks, "Those conflicts and disputes among you, where do they come from?" And James says about us, "From your cravings, your wanting, your coveting, your wrong asking, your friendship with the world, your pride."

It is fitting that Jesus gives his second summary of his sacrifice just before pointing up this sin of wanting to be the greatest. He came to change us, to alter our constant craving for greatness. And his method was to welcome us, no matter what we were like, to make himself the servant of all, to be last and least, so that we could be forgiven and made first.

Oh, of course ... you say that Jesus made the easy choice? He took a little child ... everyone can love a baby. And if I told you how that child grew up, if I told you that he was neglected at home, abused by companions, that he fell into bad company and became a brigand and was himself crucified, and if I told you that there on the cross this Jesus took him again — not into his arms, for they were nailed to his own cross — but took him into his forgiving embrace and promised him, "Today you will be with me in paradise" — if I told you that, would you still excuse yourself from welcoming all those whom the Lord welcomes? Would you, if I told you that? Of course, I can't tell you that. We do not now how that child turned out. But we do know that this Jesus never turned away *any*. This Jesus welcomed all. This Jesus was the servant of all. This Jesus was the greatest.

And this Jesus has made each one of us great. This Jesus has welcomed us. The Father who sent him has welcomed us. And each one of us can become greater than we are, than we have been. All that God has done in Christ Jesus' agony and resurrection has worked together for good for us. For we love God. We are called according to his purpose. Day by day we are being the more conformed to the image of Christ's greatness. We know more and more that we are within a large family of the welcomed. The Holy Trinity has taken us up in the arms of Holy Baptism and has placed us among the family of the Church. "You're welcome!" God says. "You can welcome," God says.

"Lord, I would be selfless. Help Thou my selfishness!"

You are able. You're a big child now. You have the wisdom. "The wisdom from above is first pure, then peaceable, gentle, willing to yield, full of mercy and good fruits, without a trace of partiality or hypocrisy. And a harvest of righteousness is sown in peace for those who make peace."

Welcome him now, him who welcomes you to his table. "Come up higher," he says.

"After you," we say. "We follow after you!"

---

1. Ngaio Marsh, *Vintage Murder* (Boston: Little, Brown and Company, 1972), pp. 43-44. First published in England in 1937.

Mark 9:38-50 (C)   Proper 21
Mark 9:38-43, 45, 47-48 (RC)   Pentecost 19
                                            Ordinary Time 26

Children
Just Forever

You are now, each one of you, and you have always been since you were baptized, one of these "little ones" who believe. Since the name of Christ was laid on you, and you were marked with his cross, he has claimed you as one of his "little ones" of which the text speaks, "these little ones who believe in me." At the time Jesus said these words there were only "little ones" for Jesus had not been around long enough to have big ones, people who had been believers in him for a lifetime, or for half a lifetime. In any case, to the eyes of God, and to the eyes of the Son of God, all of us mortals must seem to be little, to be "little ones."

The point of all this is that even as one of Christ's little ones you are big enough to know the facts of life. There are "stumbling blocks" which can be big enough to shake the faith of believers, and these stumbling blocks may be on your pathway. There is a possibility that little ones on "the way" may stumble. This text states that fact as a warning. There are people who, because they are evil, or because they simply don't care about the Father or the Son, may deliberately or carelessly put such stumbling blocks in the path of the children.

The text warns such people against causing a little one to stumble. "If any one of you put a stumbling block before one of these little ones who believe in me, it would be better for you if a great millstone were hung around your neck and you were thrown into the sea."

But you're a big girl now. You're a big boy now. You have matured. Does that mean you can look out for yourself, you do not have to be careful? Back then Jesus took a little child in his arms and used it for his welcoming illustration. Then, no doubt, he handed the child back to the parents. Your parents not only took you up in their arms and presented you to God in Holy Baptism, but they also took you back, took you home. They made sure that you grew in faith and in the knowledge of Jesus Christ. From a child you have known the sacred writings that have instructed you for salvation through faith in Christ Jesus (2 Timothy 3:15). As a child of God you have been "sealed by the Holy Spirit and marked with the cross of Christ forever." This is also true about those of you who have been baptized as adults, although the sequence may have been different. In either case, fellow "little ones," you who are big boys now, big girls now, you should face up to this fact of your lives, the fact that you might cause *your own self* to stumble.

What then? If the preferred treatment of deep sea drowning is prescribed for the stumbler, what about the fate of the stumblee? That comes clear in the next verses. They spell out direct warnings to each one of us little ones. Your own hand might cause you to stumble, your own foot, your own eye. Without anyone pushing you, you might wobble on the way. That means you may fail in faith. A great millstone and the deep sea are the preferred treatment for those who cause stumbling. What does our Lord's warning tell us of the fate of those who trip up themselves?

A reward is promised to the faithful, to those who do the good works of faith, like giving a cup of cold water to someone who bears the name of Christ. Jesus even reaches out to those who do good works of power in his name who are not part of his group of followers. "Whoever is not against us is for us." And their reward? This text does not describe it, but merely says they will "by no means lose the reward." Previously Jesus had said that anyone who welcomes a little child in his name also is welcoming him, and then added that actually it is God the Father who sent him who is welcomed. Their reward, then, is everything that could be imagined from living with God as a welcomed guest in one's life. It would include all earthly divine companionship and all heavenly blessedness. That's easy to take.

But what about those who fall by their own carelessness by the wayside? What will be the result for those who stumble? You're a big boy now; you're a big girl now. The alternative that lies before those who stumble is a place where "their worm never dies, and the fire is never quenched." It's hell, little ones.

The modern mind would discount all this, especially the graphic details. But just as a reward of being *with* God is as good as it gets, so the result of stumbles and ultimately a final fall is being *without* God. And that is as bad as it gets. Our only wise conclusion must be, "Don't stumble. Don't fall." We are not able to control all the forces of evil that would trip us up; but we should surely heed the warning, "Don't trip yourself up." The last words of this text speak to this warning: "For everyone will be salted with fire. Salt is good; but if salt has lost its saltiness, how can you season it? Have salt in yourselves, and be at peace with one another." The probable meaning of these words is: "Discipline yourself, or be disciplined." Salt is a preservative. "Have salt in yourselves" then means "preserve yourself." There are things not to do — with your hands or your feet or your eyes. James gives us that kind of advice and spells out details. "Resist the devil. Draw near to God. Cleanse your hands. Purify your hearts. Don't judge your neighbor. Don't boast in your arrogance" (James 4:7-17). But there are also admonitions to *do* things. Take the opportunities of giving a cup of water to drink to those who bear the name of Christ, and work your way up from there. Use your hands to help, your feet to walk the extra mile, your eyes to show the way to others. Discipline yourself or prepare to be disciplined — "Be salted with fire."

This is the reality which Jesus Christ himself sets before us. It ought to give us a deeper awareness of why our Lord, our God, was so determined, so ready to endure all the burning agony and punishment of hell for us, was so unstumbling in walking the way of righteousness in vicarious obedience for us. "From all sin, from all error, from all evil; from the cunning assaults of the devil; from an unprepared and evil death," we pray in the litany, "Good Lord, deliver us." Our Lord has. But evil still *is*, within and without. Our prayer, "Deliver us from evil," seeks continual help against the forces that would fell us and against our own weaknesses that would cause us to fall.

What chance do we have, we whose hearts fail for fear, whose strength wanes, who shuffle along the way, scarcely getting one foot in front of the other, always in danger of stumbling, often stumbling and falling? You are, we are, big children of God now, it's true. But to God, remember, we are always the "little ones" who believe. How do we get back to innocence when over and over again we stumble into un-faith and un-worthiness? How can we who have taken the big falls get back to being the little ones of God? When once we have stumbled — and we have over and over again — what use to cry, "Out, damned spot! Out, I say." "All the perfumes of Arabia will not sweeten" our hands, or our feet, or our eyes. How hollow sounds the claim, "Every day in every way I am getting better and better." How much more realistic, although even more impossible for us, are the lines from Eizabeth Akers Allen:

Backwards, turn backwards, O Time, in your flight,
Make me a child again just for tonight.

Matthew's account of this gospel ends with the words, "It is not the will of your Father in heaven that one of these little ones should be lost" (Matthew 18:14). None of us little ones wants that either. But the mystery of "why some, not others" remains. Think of Judas and be very sober about this. Think of Peter and be saved.

Judas thought he could betray and still be Christ's disciple. Jesus knew and Jesus let Judas know that he knew: "One of you will betray me." Judas was warned. Jesus said, "It is the one to whom I will give this piece of bread when I have dipped it into the dish." He gave it to Judas. "He immediately went out. And it was night" (John 13:21-30). Just ... tonight ... Jesus tried to make Judas a child again that night, to make him just again. Judas would not.

Jesus knew and let Peter know that he knew what even Peter did not know. Peter was warned. When the cock crowed and Peter had denied him three times, Jesus looked through the night and his eyes found Peter's. Peter remembered. Peter wept bitterly. And Jesus made Peter a child again that very night.

Judas cried, too, but not as a little one cries. Who can understand his error? What we must focus on is God's offered love, a love that moves us to tears and back to childhood. God has made a way for each of us, no matter what the stumble, to become a child again. What do *you* do when your child comes weeping bitterly, wishing that what has been done might be undone, sobbing, "Backwards, turn backwards, O Time in your flight"? You hug your child. You weep with your child. You love your child. God deals with us as his children, his little ones. Be hugged. Accept his love. Come home again. Be a child again, God's little one.

And do not forget: God accepts help. James writes, "You should know that whoever brings back a sinner from wandering will save the sinner's soul from death and will cover a multitude of sins." He urges us wanderers from the truth, "Confess your sins to one another, and pray for one another. The prayer of the righteous is powerful and effective" (James 5:20, 16). And as God picks us up from where we have fallen, we can add a word: "The prayer of the *made righteous* is powerful and effective."

Even on the night in which Judas betrayed him, Jesus showed the love of God for us all. Even before he gave his body and his blood on the cross, he gave them to us with the bread and wine of the last supper. In the upper room he prayed the Father to keep those disciples, to keep all of us, safe, to keep us from the evil one. He said to them, "I have said these things to you to keep you from stumbling" (John 16:1). That night they all did stumble. But after his resurrection he appeared to some of the disciples before breakfast on the shore where they had been fishing. He asked them, "Children, you have no fish, have you?" It was more statement than question. They had not. Then the miracle of the great draft of fish. He comes to us, too, after our times of stumbling and weeping. He knows; he says, "You have no strength, no saltiness, have you?" He has no need of an answer. He performs the greatest of miracles, our restoration as God's little ones, God's children.

All he asked of Peter, of all the disciples, all he asks of us, is "Lovest thou me?" And, as if time has turned backward, all is as it has been before: he our Lord, we his faithful followers.

He turns backwards, turns backwards, time in its flight. He makes us, each one of us, his child again, not just for a night, but, just, forever!

Lectionary Preaching After Pentecost

Virtually all pastors who make use of the sermons in this book will find their worship life and planning shaped by one of two lectionary series. Most mainline Protestant denominations, along with clergy of the Roman Catholic Church, have now approved — either for provisional or official use — the three-year Revised Common (Consensus) Lectionary. This family of denominations includes United Methodist, Presbyterian, United Church of Christ and Disciples of Christ. Recently the ELCA division of Lutheranism also began following the Revised Common Lectionary. This change has been reflected in the headings and scripture listings with each sermon in this book.

Roman Catholics and Lutheran divisions other than ELCA follow their own three-year cycle of texts. While there are divergences between the Revised Common and Roman Catholic/Lutheran systems, the gospel texts show striking parallels, with few text selections evidencing significant differences. Nearly all the gospel texts included in this book will, therefore, be applicable to worship and preaching planning for clergy following either lectionary.

A significant divergence does occur, however, in the method by which specific gospel texts are assigned to specific calendar days. The Revised Common and Roman Catholic Lectionaries accomplish this by counting backwards from Christ the King (Last Sunday after Pentecost), discarding "extra" texts from the front of the list: Lutherans (not using the Revised Common Lectionary) follow the opposite pattern, counting forward from The Holy Trinity, discarding "extra" texts at the end of the list.

The following index will aid the user of this book in matching the correct text to the correct Sunday during the Pentecost portion of the church year.

(Fixed dates do not pertain to Lutheran Lectionary)

Fixed Date Lectionaries *Revised Common (including ELCA)* *and Roman Catholic*	Lutheran Lectionary *Lutheran*
The Day of Pentecost	The Day of Pentecost
The Holy Trinity	The Holy Trinity
May 29-June 4 — Proper 4, Ordinary Time 9	Pentecost 2
June 5-11 — Proper 5, Ordinary Time 10	Pentecost 3
June 12-18 — Proper 6, Ordinary Time 11	Pentecost 4

June 19-25 — Proper 7, Ordinary Time 12	Pentecost 5
June 26-July 2 — Proper 8, Ordinary Time 13	Pentecost 6
July 3-9 — Proper 9, Ordinary Time 14	Pentecost 7
July 10-16 — Proper 10, Ordinary Time 15	Pentecost 8
July 17-23 — Proper 11, Ordinary Time 16	Pentecost 9
July 24-30 — Proper 12, Ordinary Time 17	Pentecost 10
July 31-Aug. 6 — Proper 13, Ordinary Time 18	Pentecost 11
Aug. 7-13 — Proper 14, Ordinary Time 19	Pentecost 12
Aug. 14-20 — Proper 15, Ordinary Time 20	Pentecost 13
Aug. 21-27 — Proper 16, Ordinary Time 21	Pentecost 14
Aug. 28-Sept. 3 — Proper 17, Ordinary Time 22	Pentecost 15
Sept. 4-10 — Proper 18, Ordinary Time 23	Pentecost 16
Sept. 11-17 — Proper 19, Ordinary Time 24	Pentecost 17
Sept. 18-24 — Proper 20, Ordinary Time 25	Pentecost 18
Sept. 25-Oct. 1 — Proper 21, Ordinary Time 26	Pentecost 19
Oct. 2-8 — Proper 22, Ordinary Time 27	Pentecost 20
Oct. 9-15 — Proper 23, Ordinary Time 28	Pentecost 21
Oct. 16-22 — Proper 24, Ordinary Time 29	Pentecost 22
Oct. 23-29 — Proper 25, Ordinary Time 30	Pentecost 23
Oct. 30-Nov. 5 — Proper 26, Ordinary Time 31	Pentecost 24
Nov. 6-12 — Proper 27, Ordinary Time 32	Pentecost 25
Nov. 13-19 — Proper 28, Ordinary Time 33	Pentecost 26
	Pentecost 27
Nov. 20-26 — Christ the King	Christ the King

Reformation Day (or last Sunday in October) is October 31 (Revised Common, Lutheran)

All Saints' Day (or first Sunday in November) is November 1 (Revised Common, Lutheran, Roman Catholic)

Books In This Cycle B Series

Gospel Set

God's Downward Mobility
Sermons For Advent, Christmas And Epiphany
John A. Stroman

Which Way To Jesus?
Sermons For Lent And Easter
Harry N. Huxhold

Water Won't Quench The Fire
Sermons For Pentecost (First Third)
William G. Carter

Fringe, Front And Center
Sermons For Pentecost (Middle Third)
George W. Hoyer

No Box Seats In The Kingdom
Sermons For Pentecost (Last Third)
William G. Carter

First Lesson Set

Light In The Land Of Shadows
Sermons For Advent, Christmas And Epiphany
Harold C. Warlick, Jr.

Times Of Refreshing
Sermons For Lent and Easter
E. Carver McGriff

Lyrics For The Centuries
Sermons For Pentecost (First Third)
Arthur H. Kolsti

No Particular Place To Go
Sermons For Pentecost (Middle Third)
Timothy J. Smith

When Trouble Comes!
Sermons For Pentecost (Last Third)
Zan W. Holmes, Jr.

www.ingramcontent.com/pod-product-compliance
Lightning Source LLC
Chambersburg PA
CBHW071735040426
42446CB00012B/2362